Compassion Focused Group Therapy for the Severely Mentally Ill

This workbook should be used alongside *A Clinician's Guide to Compassion Focused Group Therapy for the Severely Mentally Ill* to aid participants throughout their group journey in compassion focused therapy (CFT). CFT is a type of therapy aimed at understanding, alleviating, and preventing suffering in oneself and others.

Divided into 12 modules, group members will move through the content with the support of their therapist. It is designed to be used during and between group sessions. Participants will be able to access and review key pieces of information. Additionally, participants will be able to engage with group material by completing handouts and applying CFT to their own life. Out of session practices can also be found inside, to further support patients in their growth.

This is an ideal resource for patients in an inpatient setting, experiencing self-criticism and shame.

Aileen Rands, MS, is a doctoral candidate with over five years of working with SMI individuals. She is currently completing her pre-doctoral internship at a Veteran Affairs Administration. She is an emerging psychologist with an interest in severe psychopathology and group psychotherapy.

Doug Benson, PsyD, DBT-LBC, is a psychologist with 20 years of experience working with SMI. He is board-certified in DBT, a clinical supervisor for Utah State Hospitals psychology internship/postdoc, develops treatment programming, participates in clinical research in conjunction with Brigham Young University, and provides clinical services.

Amanda L. Rapacz, PsyD, has worked for the State of Utah in the Department of Health and Human Services at Utah State Hospital since 2009 and is currently the Assistant Superintendent. She is the licensed psychologist serving on the State of Utah's Division of Professional Licensing Behavioral Health Board. Her passion for the field of psychology and working with individuals who have severe and persistent mental illness has led to presidential positions on the Utah Psychological Association and NAMI-Utah boards.

Gary Burlingame, PhD, has 40+ years of training, teaching, and research experience on effective group therapies, recognized by USA and international professional associations. He began focusing on outpatient SMI treatment in the 1990s, with 25 years of service developing inpatient group programming. He is the past president of the American Group Psychotherapy Association and the Society of Group Psychology and Group Psychotherapy.

Compassion Focused Group Therapy for the Severely Mentally Ill

A Participant's Workbook

Aileen Rands, Doug Benson,
Amanda L. Rapacz, and
Gary Burlingame

Routledge
Taylor & Francis Group

NEW YORK AND LONDON

Designed cover image: © Getty Images

First published 2026
by Routledge
605 Third Avenue, New York, NY 10158

and by Routledge
4 Park Square, Milton Park, Abingdon, Oxon, OX14 4RN

Routledge is an imprint of the Taylor & Francis Group, an informa business

© 2026 Aileen Rands, Doug Benson, Amanda L. Rapacz, and
Gary Burlingame

The right of Aileen Rands, Doug Benson, Amanda L. Rapacz, and
Gary Burlingame to be identified as authors of this work has
been asserted in accordance with sections 77 and 78 of the
Copyright, Designs and Patents Act 1988.

ISBN: 978-1-003-86391-5 (hbk)
ISBN: 978-1-003-86390-8 (pbk)
ISBN: 978-1-003-60756-4 (ebk)

DOI: 10.4324/9781003607564

Typeset in Sabon
by Apex CoVantage, LLC

Contents

Introduction and Welcome

Welcome to compassion focused therapy (CFT), we are glad you decided to join a group. We are honored to be a part of your healing journey. CFT pulls together wisdom humans around the world have had for thousands of years. CFT also pulls together recent research on how our bodies and brains work.

The first thing for you to know is what we mean when we say compassion. Sometimes people start this group and think compassion is a weakness or being soft or a waste of time. In this group you are going to learn that compassion is something completely different. Compassion is about building courage, gaining wisdom, and working through things that have caused us pain and suffering. By learning about and practicing compassion you will feel less criticism, shame, anger, and resentment. Compassion is a skill set, or ability, that we can build and strengthen. In this group we are taking small steps to build this compassion muscle.

This workbook has been developed to be used during your group sessions with your therapist. It is divided into 12 modules that you will move through in order. You will find information on the things you learn in group and handouts to fill out. This workbook will be helpful to use between group sessions, as you practice. Your group therapist will answer any questions you might have.

Fears of Coming to Therapy

We know that being in a new therapy can feel uncomfortable, awkward, or even frightening. You might be thinking: what's going to happen in this group? Will I like my group leader? I feel scared to participate. I don't know anyone else in group. Will this even help me? It is important to keep in mind that these thoughts and feelings are normal and you are not alone! You can share these feelings in group and work through them. Your group leaders will do all they can to help you so you keep coming back. It's a courageous act that you are already doing in coming along.

DOI: 10.4324/9781003607564-1

As you stick with this group you will lean that you have more in common than you think with everyone in the group. As humans we all have tricky brains, feel difficult emotions, and painful experiences in our past. Group therapy is a powerful space to learn from others, help others, connect, and grow together. You group leader will help you do this. We recommend you do your best to share your story and practice what you learn in group.

Introduction, Compassion, and Tricky Brain

Aims:

- Get to know each other and talk about group rules.
- Look at what compassion is and is not.
- Understand our tricky brains, and understand that our brains are not our fault but are our responsibility.
- Finish with an exercise to start practicing compassionate.

DOI: 10.4324/9781003607564-2

compassion is empathy in action

tricky brain

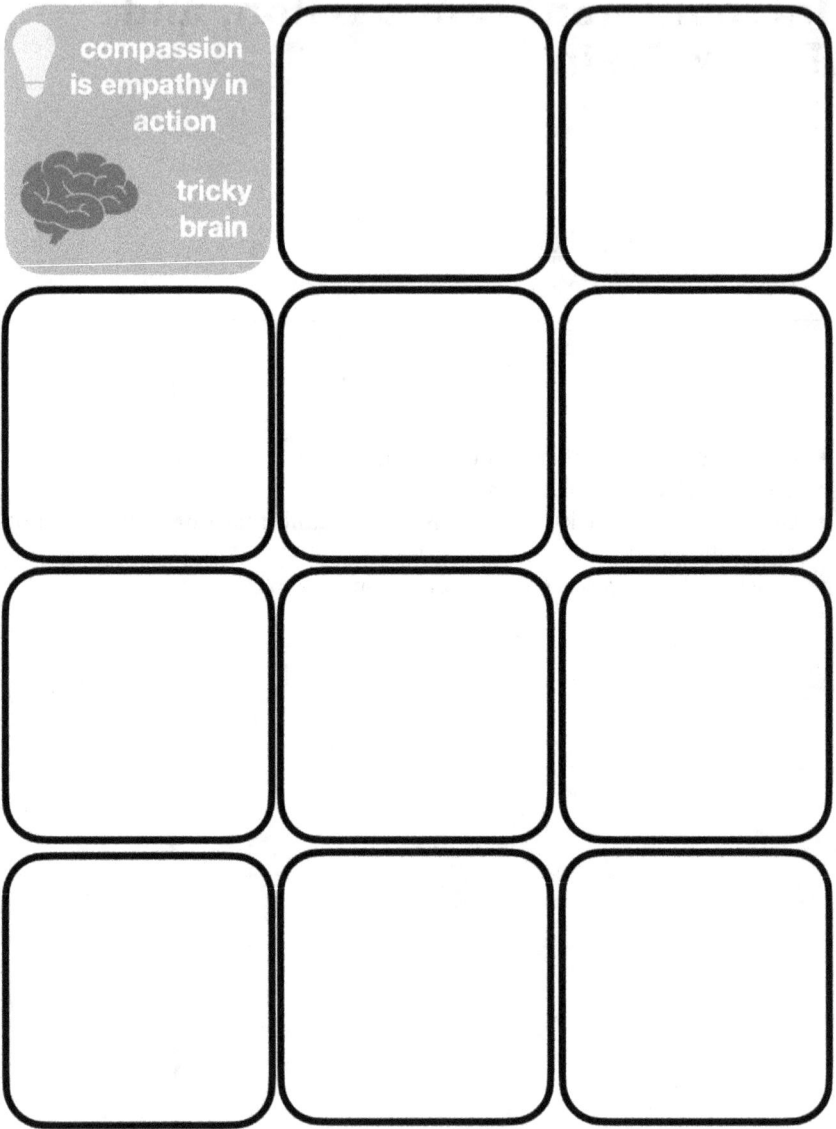

Figure 1 A visual representation of module 1 of 12.

Introduction

In our CFT group we will learn about the body and the mind and how they interact with others. In each session we'll be spending a little time learning some important CFT skills. We expect that you will practice the skills and exercises we cover in group outside of group.

Our goal in this group is to increase wisdom and understanding of how our brain and past experiences affect us. In each group we want to help you to apply the content and skills to your own personal life outside of group. In short, we want to hear from you about how CFT is working or not working for you so that our group is personally relevant.

What Is Compassion?

Today we talked about what compassion is and is not. We will continue to talk about these three qualities through our group.

Remember that compassion is *not*:

- Just being nice
- Feeling sorry for other people
- Being submissive
- Just about love
- Weak

Compassion is:

1. Wisdom
2. Strength
3. Commitment

"Sensitivity to suffering and distress in self and others with a commitment to try to alleviate and prevent it."

One insightful group member in another group summarized all this as "empathy in action."

Sometimes, to better understand what compassion is, it can be useful to think about very compassionate people you know. What makes them compassionate? What do they do and say? How do these people act?

Turn to Handout 1.2 to review what compassion is and is not. Add your own thoughts on what compassion is and is not.

Our Tricky Brain, Genes, and Evolution

Wisdom is based on understanding and knowledge. The more we know about our minds and why they are the way they are, the more we can engage with suffering and work out what to do.

We all have a tricky brain, that lead to ups and downs in life. Our brain was built for us, not by us. We have genes we did not choose and do not get to control. We are socially shaped, by our experiences. While it's not our fault that our minds are like they are, it is our responsibility. It's our responsibility to learn how to work with our minds.

Our tricky brains lead us to develop thinking loops that oftentimes are not very helpful. This tricky brain can get us stuck thinking about negative things and focusing on threats. Remember, this is not our fault, but it is our responsibility.

In group we talked about a zebra running away from a lion. Once they get away and can't see, hear, or smell the lion, there is nothing to keep them anxious. In fact, they settle down quite quickly. While a human will also be relieved to escape a lion, we tend to have thoughts. We might think, "Can you imagine if I'd been caught and what would it be like to be eaten by a lion!" Our minds can overthink and create many frightening possibilities. Zebras don't do anything like this!

One of the goals of CFT is to recognize that our brain is tricky. We need to start looking at the ways we get stuck in patterns of thinking and feeling that are unhelpful. We are working toward choosing the version we want to become. We hope to develop the compassionate version of ourselves.

One of the first steps we can take is gaining compassionate wisdom. Our compassionate wisdom is knowing everything we learned about in this module. We are all here with a very tricky brain and life experiences that we didn't choose. This is part of what it means to be human. Compassionate wisdom reminds us that we are not alone.

We will continue to review and revisit this compassionate wisdom thorough group. Handout 1.3 provides a summary of this wisdom.

The Mind-Body Connection

In this group we will explore the connection between our minds and bodies. This connection is important and powerful. For example, imagine biting into a lemon, focus on how that would taste and feel in your mouth (illustrated in Handout 1.4). Maybe you salivate, your muscles tense, your lips purse . . .

This simple example highlights how our mind and body are interconnected. When we think or imagine in our minds, our bodies react. This will be important moving forward as we explore emotions more in-depth.

Group Rules

Respect & Support

- We respect each other and the courage of coming here.
- We try to support each other as best as we can.

Participation

- No pressure to talk if you don't want to.
- If someone is feeling upset, it is okay for us to focus on that before moving on.

Confidentiality

- We agree to keep things only in the group so members can feel safe.
- Remember limits of confidentiality.

Be Open Minded

- We will be open to each others differences.
- We want to make new experiences, so we try to be open to learning.

Between Session Practices

- Practice outside of session is important.
- We will begin each session with a check-in with how your between session practice went.

Other Group Rules

_____

_____

_____

_____

_____

Handout 1.1 Group Rules

Definition of Compassion

Compassion IS...

...wisdom

...strength

...commitment

...a sensitivity to suffering and distress with a commitment to alleviate and prevent it

...empathy in action

Compassion is NOT...

...not just being nice

...not feeling sorry for others

...not being submissive

...not just for people we love

...not weak

Handout 1.2 Definition of Compassion

The Tricky Brain

Flow of Life

Like all living beings, we are part of the flow of life.

Human Brain

We have a brain we did not choose, but it was developed through thousands of years of evolution.

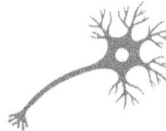

New Brain

Our brains have the capacity to do amazing things—but it can also be difficult.

Shaped

We are shaped by the environment we grew up in, which we did not choose.

Not Your Fault

The brain is tricky because it can get caught in loops. However, we can take responsibility for it using wisdom.

Handout 1.3 The Tricky Brain

The Mind-Body Connection

What happens in our mind will impact our body.

Imagine biting into a lemon…

Handout 1.4 The Mind-Body Connection

Reviewing Compassion Process

We will be talking about a made-up person named Jordan to apply what we have learned in group to real-life.

One day, Jordan was sitting out in the dayroom when a fight broke out between a new patient and another patient. With all the commotion, it was unclear who started the fight and who was involved once staff showed up. The new patient blamed Jordan, as well as everyone else in the dayroom. The nurse decided everyone present would receive consequences and decided to drop everyone's level.

What have we learned in this module that might help Jordan?

Notes

Between-Session Practice

How do we define compassion? Compassion is a sensitivity to suffering, with a commitment to alleviate and prevent it. We do exercises to help us with our goal to increase compassion.

Now let's move into an exercise. As we will talk about in group later, breathing is a tool we can use. As we slow down and focus on our breath, we slow our minds and our bodies down. This helps us move into a state where we are more open to compassion.

We start by closing our eyes or looking down. Notice how it feels to sit on your chair right now (15 seconds).

Notice your posture with your back straight and shoulders in line with your hips. Now slow your breath. Try to breathe from your stomach rather than your chest. With each slower and deeper breath say, with a friendly tone, "mind slowing down" and then "body slowing down." Alternate these phrases on each in and out breath. Gradually get that sense of grounding with a sense of stilling and slowing, but also with alertness in your mind. Notice yourself becoming more grounded.

Allow time for this to settle in. (Longer pause.)

Just connect with the body. Feel your body in the chair at this moment. When you are ready, you can slowly start to come back into the room and open your eyes. (Pause.)

How was that exercise? When might an exercise like this be helpful to you? (Give time to respond.)

Module 2

Three Systems of Emotion

Aims:

- Learn about soft-landing exercises.
- Review the three systems of emotion: threat (red), drive (blue), and soothing (green).
- Explore the function of the three systems and how compassion fits in.

DOI: 10.4324/9781003607564-3

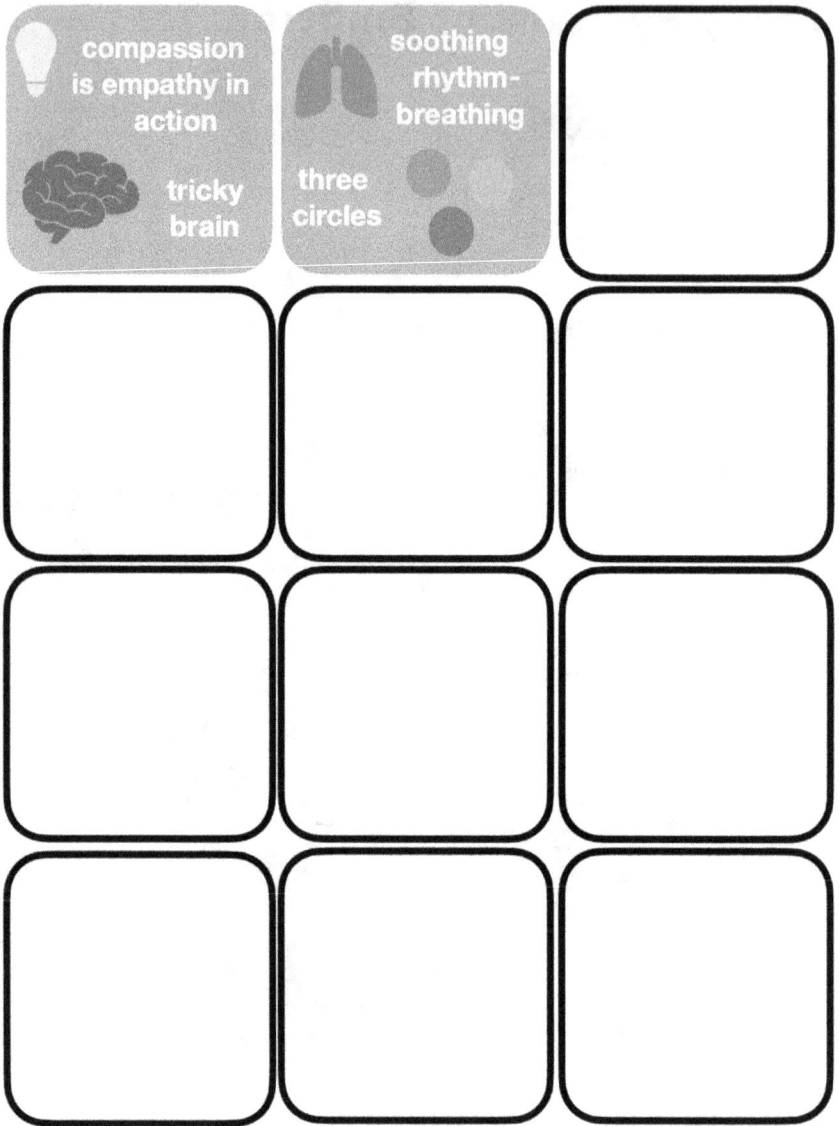

Figure 2 A visual representation of module 2 of 12.

Introduction

In this module, we are going to look at our three emotion systems. These three systems have evolved to help us survive and thrive. Thrive means we can accomplish our goals and improve.

Three Emotion Systems

The first system is the **threat system**. The threat system *helps us deal with things that might be dangerous or harmful.*

The second is the **drive system**. The drive system is *actively moving toward things that are good for us. That will help us compete and thrive or succeed.*

The third is the **soothing system**. The soothing system is *a sense of peace and relaxation. It is feeling connected to the world and other people.*

In our group we will be describing these three systems with the three-circle model (illustrated in Handout 2.1). It labels the threat system as the "red circle," the drive system as the "blue circle," and the soothing system as the "green circle."

Just because emotions connected with these systems are built in doesn't mean that they are easy to manage. The feelings can be uncomfortable and confusing. They may even happen at the same time. Emotions are complicated and difficult. This difficulty sometimes makes us want to get rid of certain emotions. However, all emotions are there to help you survive and thrive. They are important to your existence. We need them. So, in this module, we will look at how these emotions play out in our bodies, in our minds, and in our behaviors. We will explore ways to develop balance between the three emotion systems.

Threat (Red) Circle

The red circle represents the threat system, which includes emotions such as anxiety, fear, and anger. The threat system tells us when we need to be alert. We feel these emotions in our bodies to help us stay safe and avoid danger. The threat system is automatic. This system works very quickly. The threat system has its advantages and disadvantages. One major disadvantage is that we tend to notice and remember bad things more than we do good things. We focus on threats more quickly, we remember threats more than we remember soothing, and we hold onto threats. Yet we must remember that the red circle is also good, as it attempts to keep us safe.

Complete Handouts 2.2 and 2.3 to see how you experience the threat emotions of anxiety and anger. These emotions impact our body, attention/thinking, and behavior.

Drive (Blue) Circle

The blue circle is our drive system. It includes positive emotions that work to succeeding in life rather than avoiding danger. Like threat emotions, these positive emotions effect our body and attention. Emotions in this system can drive competition. Sometimes our threat system and our drive system mix. This leads to thoughts like "We are only good enough if we live up to what others expect." Instead of our emotions driving us to do something that makes us feel good about ourselves, we can shut down or avoid doing something because of threat emotions. This pattern can make it hard to learn how to cope with the ups and downs of life.

Complete Handout 2.4 to see how you experience the drive emotion of excitement. This emotion impacts our body, attention/thinking, and behavior.

Soothing (Green) Circle

The green circle, or soothing system, is also connected to positive emotions. When animals are not under threat, they can go into a state of restfulness or calming (remember the zebra example). This is important. As our body slows down, the mind and body are able to rest and recover. Soothing emotions help to balance the other emotions. They help us to feel safe, explore, and be creative. This helps us make rational decisions. We need our soothing system to balance the threat and drive systems. Most of us spend most of our time in the other emotions systems, so we need to practice being in our soothing system.

It's important to remember that we don't want to get rid of any of these systems. Each of them has an important role. What we want to do is find a balance between the systems. Notice if your three systems are currently balanced or imbalanced (reference Handout 2.6).

Complete Handout 2.5 to see how you experience the soothing emotion of peace. This emotion impacts our body, attention/thinking, and behavior.

Soothing Rhythm-Breathing

Let's think about how our body reacts to the different emotion systems. You may have noticed that some are related to stimulating the body. Others are related to calming the body.

Our **sympathetic nervous system** is the system in the brain that acts like the gas, it gets us going. It is threat and drive. Our **parasympathetic system** acts as the brakes. It is soothing. Ideally, these two systems should work in balance. Although we're interested in balance, what you may have noticed is that your soothing system isn't working as well as you want. We can concentrate on that and begin to train it—to exercise the soothing system. One way to improve parasympathetic functioning is through soothing rhythm-breathing. You can find instructions for soothing rhythm-breathing at the end of this module.

The 3 Circle Model

Each emotion system is important. Compassion helps us to balance our circles.

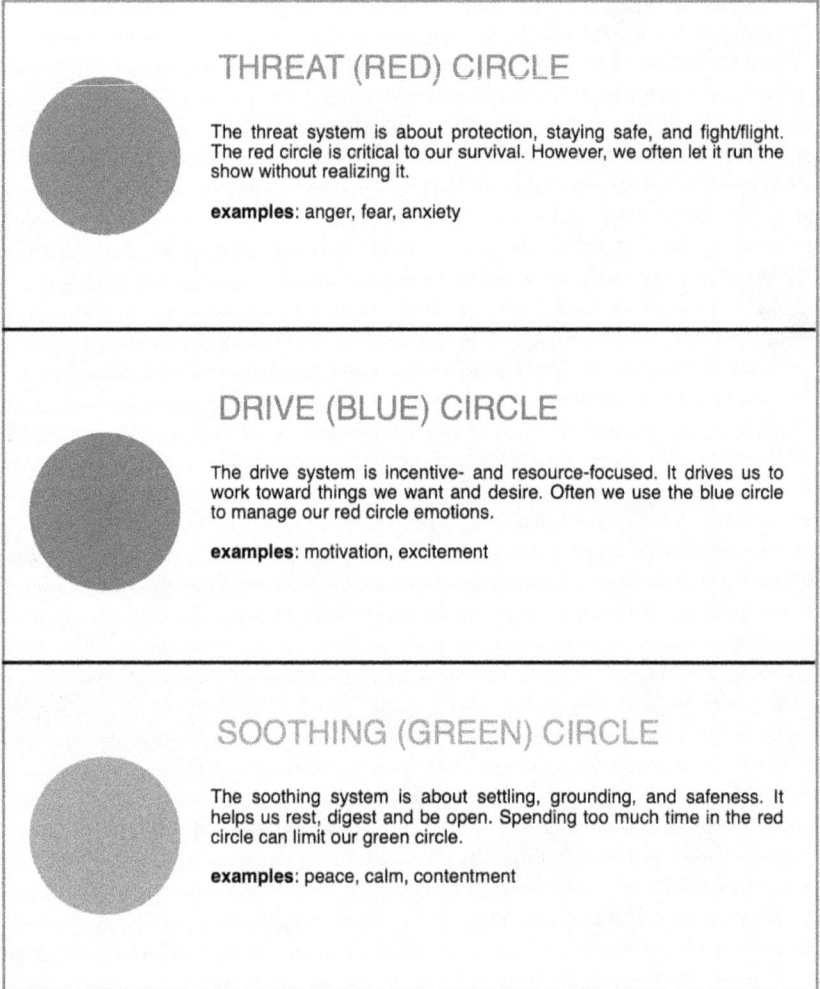

THREAT (RED) CIRCLE

The threat system is about protection, staying safe, and fight/flight. The red circle is critical to our survival. However, we often let it run the show without realizing it.

examples: anger, fear, anxiety

DRIVE (BLUE) CIRCLE

The drive system is incentive- and resource-focused. It drives us to work toward things we want and desire. Often we use the blue circle to manage our red circle emotions.

examples: motivation, excitement

SOOTHING (GREEN) CIRCLE

The soothing system is about settling, grounding, and safeness. It helps us rest, digest and be open. Spending too much time in the red circle can limit our green circle.

examples: peace, calm, contentment

Handout 2.1 The Three-Circle Model

The Function of Anxiety

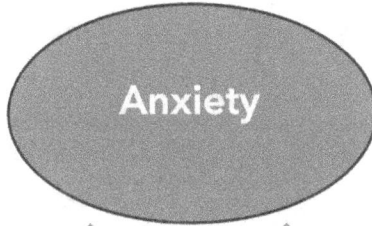

Anxiety

Body
- Tense muscles
- Heart rate increase
- Sweat
  _____
  _____
  _____

Attention/Thinking
- Narrow-focus
- Racing thoughts
- Rumination
  _____
  _____
  _____

Behavior
- Avoidance
- Submission
- Dissociation
  _____
  _____
  _____

Notes:

Handout 2.2 The Function of Anxiety

The Function of Anger

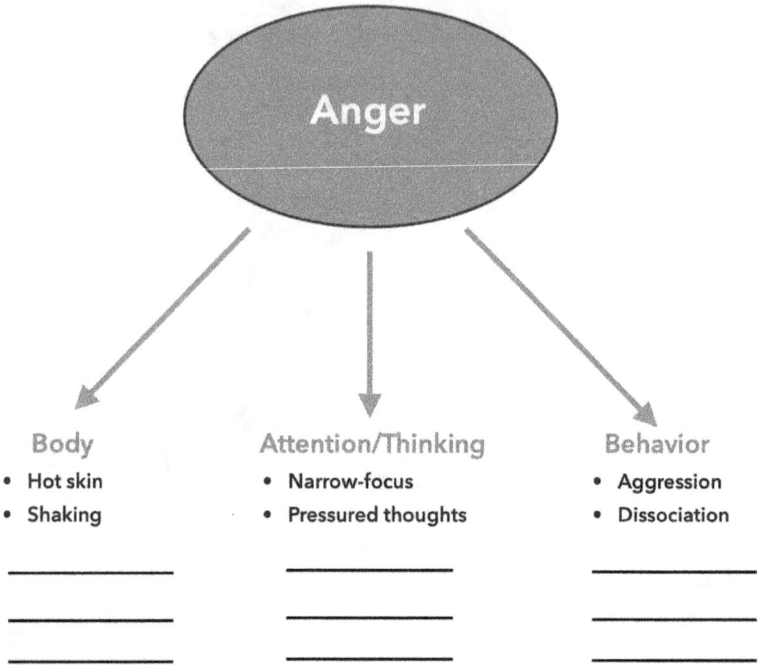

Anger

Body
- Hot skin
- Shaking

_____

_____

_____

Attention/Thinking
- Narrow-focus
- Pressured thoughts

_____

_____

_____

Behavior
- Aggression
- Dissociation

_____

_____

_____

Notes:

Handout 2.3 The Function of Anger

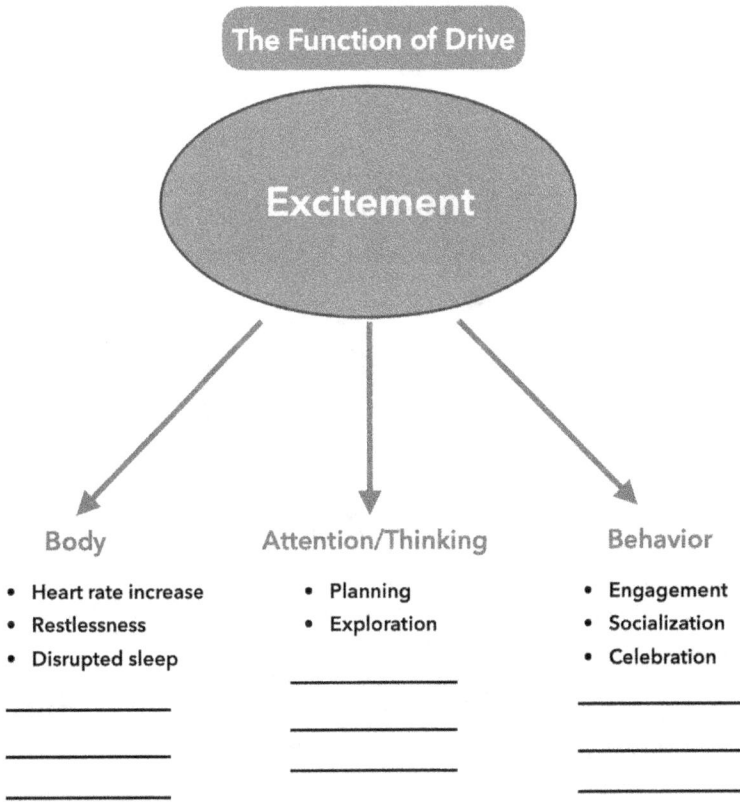

The Function of Drive

Excitement

Body
- Heart rate increase
- Restlessness
- Disrupted sleep
- _____
- _____
- _____

Attention/Thinking
- Planning
- Exploration
- _____
- _____
- _____

Behavior
- Engagement
- Socialization
- Celebration
- _____
- _____
- _____

Notes:

Handout 2.4 The Function of Drive

The Function of Soothing

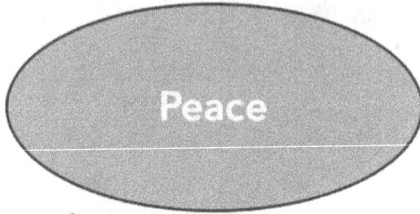

Peace

Body/Feelings

- Relaxed muscles
- Slow breathing
- Upright posture

_____

_____

_____

Attention/Thinking

- Clear Mind
- Thoughtfulness
- Kindness

_____

_____

_____

Behavior

- Gentleness
- Friendliness
- Helpfulness

_____

_____

_____

Notes:

Handout 2.5 The Function of Peace

Draw Your Own 3 Circles

* Which circle do you spend the most time in?
* Which circle do you spend the least time in?
* Are your 3 circles balanced OR imbalanced?

Handout 2.6 Draw Your Own Three Circles

Reviewing Compassion Process

> Module 1: Dayroom fight, level drop, anger/anxiety, thinking loops; trick brain, "not my fault but my responsibility"

Let's think of how to apply what we have learned today to Jordan's situation. When Jordan's level was dropped, he got angry. He was in the red circle, or the threat circle.

What have we learned in this module that might help Jordan?

Notes

Between-Session Practice

Soothing Rhythm Breathing

Find a comfortable sitting position and notice how it feels to sit in your chair. (Pause.)

Now, we will engage our compassionate body posture.

1. Sit with a straight back. Keep your head upright and your shoulders in line with your hips. Place your feet flat on the floor.
2. Lift your shoulders up and slightly backward.
3. Find a comfortable position for your hands that will not be distracting to you.
4. Breathe into your belly rather than your chest.
5. Bring a friendly facial expression to your body posture.
6. Gently fix your gaze on a single spot on the floor or close your eyes if you feel comfortable.

If you notice yourself getting distracted from what I'm asking you to pay attention to, that's okay, and it is part of what our brain does. Just compassionately bring yourself back to my voice.

First, notice how you breathe naturally. Pay attention to how breathing makes you feel. Notice how the air comes down into your lungs and then out again. Notice your posture while still focusing on your breathing. (Pause.)

Now let's try to change our natural rhythm slightly. This will help activate your soothing system and create changes in your brain and body. Begin to slow and deepen your natural breath. Your breathing should remain even and unforced. Aim for about five seconds in and five seconds out. For some, counting can be helpful. For others that can get in the way. Find what works best for you.

As you develop your rhythm, notice and focus on the feeling of inner slowing with each outbreath. On each in breath, say, in your mind, "mind slowing down." On each outbreath, say "body slowing down." Continue alternating these phrases throughout the practice in your head. Maintain an alert mind even as you try to become stiller, slower, and more grounded.

As we practice for a moment, pay attention to the experience of even and unforced breathing. (Pause.)

Now, sense the weight of your body resting on the chair. You may notice that you feel heavier. Feel the stableness in your body that comes from both your compassionate posture and a slower and deeper breath. Imagine sitting like a mountain, strong and stable. Notice these feelings of weight and stability in your body. (Pause.)

This is called grounding.

You may have also noticed a sense of stilling during this practice. This feeling of stillness will grow as we continue slowing, stilling, and grounding ourselves throughout the group.

As we bring this practice of soothing rhythm-breathing to a close, connect with your body again. Feel your body in the chair in this moment. Slowly start to come back into the room, and open your eyes when you are ready.

Attention Training and Mindfulness

Aims:

- Explore these three concepts: (1) attention, (2) mindfulness, and (3) emotion labeling.
- Learn how to "pay attention" to, or focus on, our attention.
- Practice mindfulness skills, including breathing, grounding, and body awareness.
- Explore possible behaviors that help develop compassion.

DOI: 10.4324/9781003607564-4

Figure 3 A visual representation of module 3 of 12.

Introduction

This module is designed to help us learn how to direct our attention. Think of how a flashlight illuminates what it shines upon. Just like that, we can focus our attention to illuminate certain things. In this module, we'll introduce mindfulness to help you become more aware of your own attending. This model of mindfulness will help you to direct your attention in ways that will be helpful.

Attention

Attention is like a flashlight. When you focus your attention on something, you shine your mental "flashlight" onto it. When we focus on some things in our mind, other things fall out of focus. You are in charge of where your attention is directed, so it is important to practice noticing what you are focused on.

To notice where your attention is, there are questions you may ask yourself. You can ask, "Where is my attention pointing?" or "What am I focused on right now?" Our surroundings and the current moment are not the only things we can shift our attention to. We can also shift our attention toward our memories of the past, emotions, and thoughts. When we shift our attention, our body and mind change accordingly. We might need to practice noticing what is happening internally. To increase our compassion toward our personal experience, we can use breathing, grounding, and compassionate intention.

Mindfulness

We sometimes go into "automatic pilot." In automatic pilot, we do not pay attention, and we may fail to act with intent. Have you ever driven home without really remembering how you got there? Have you gotten angry and acted out in ways which you have later regretted? These are examples of automatic pilot.

Mindfulness is a skill we can use to stop ourselves from going into automatic pilot. Mindfulness allows us to be aware of our minds and to make choices with intent. Mindfulness does not mean you stay focused and never get distracted. It is normal to cycle through focus and distraction. Look at Handout 3.1 to see the cycle of mindfulness. There are many, many ways we can be mindful. Handout 3.2 lists different things you can try.

Compassionate Body Posture, Voice Tone, and Body Expression

Remember the three circles of emotion (threat, drive, and soothing). We want to be aware of what our body is doing because it is connected to these systems. Through practice, we can shift into certain body postures that help put us into a compassionate state. We can do this by becoming aware and observant of our body postures and states. It may feel strange to practice this, but it will get easier with practice.

To move into a more compassionate body posture, you can:

1. Sit with a straight back. Keep your head upright and your shoulders in line with your hips. Place your feet flat on the floor.
2. Lift your shoulders up and slightly backward.
3. Find a comfortable position for your hands that will not be distracting to you.
4. Breathe into your belly rather than your chest.
5. Bring a friendly facial expression to your body posture.
6. Keep your gaze fixed gently on a single spot on the floor or remain with your eyes closed if you feel comfortable.

Cycle of Mindfulness

Mindfulness is a practice of noticing and gently returning to the moment–NOT trying to rid one's mind of thoughts.

It helps us to become aware of what's going on in our minds and to bring our minds where we want them to be.

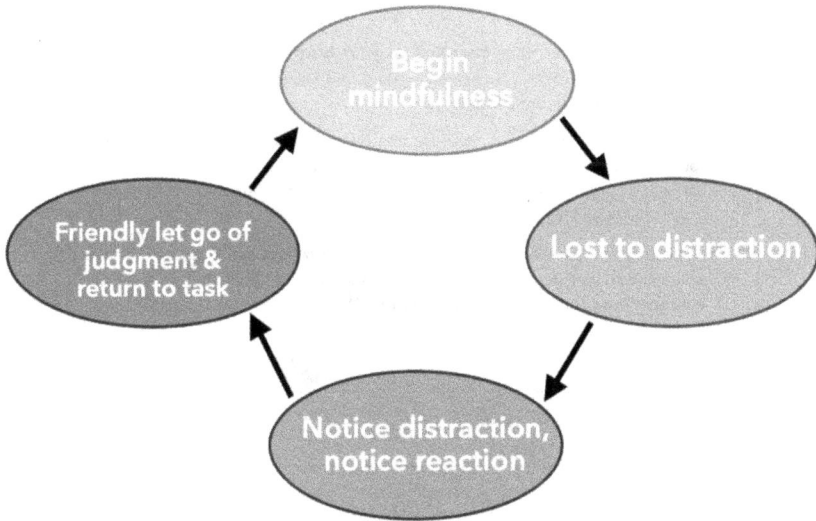

Begin mindfulness

Lost to distraction

Notice distraction, notice reaction

Friendly let go of judgment & return to task

Handout 3.1 Cycle of Mindfulness

Mindfulness Exercises

Mindful Breathing

Mindful breathing helps you to watch your breath and noticing when you get distracted.

HOW TO DO IT:

• First, get comfortable. Place your feet shoulder-width apart, flat on the ground. You might close your eyes or look down at the ground.

• Next, **gently focus your attention on your breath**. Breathe so that the air fulls your lungs. Notice your stomach rising and falling as you breathe in and out. Just notice your breath for about 30 seconds.

• REMEMBER, if your mind wanders, that is normal. The idea is to just watch your breath, and begin to notice when your attention drifts off. When you notice that your attention has left your breath, just gently bring it back to your breath, again and again, over and over.

• **The key is that when our thoughts and emotions come up, we don't judge them; we just notice them as mental events ("Oh... there's another thought") and then come back to the breath.**

(a)

Handout 3.2 Mindfulness Exercises

Mindful Eating

Mindful eating can help you to feel grounded and focus on what you are doing in the present.

• You can try this when eating any kind of food.

• First, pay attention to the food's texture and color. Take a few seconds to really examine what the food looks like. Next, feel the food, and pay attention to how it feels on your fingers. After this, smell the food and think about its smell. Last, take a bite and focus on this feeling. Think about how the food feels in your mouth and how it tastes.

Mindful Walking

Mindful walking can help you to notice your surroundings and be in the present.

•You can do this inside or outside.

• As you walk, try to notice what is around you. Slowly look up, down, and all around you. As you explore, you can pick things up and observe them. Notice how the place you are in looks, smells, sounds, and feels. Try to use as many senses as you can. As always, there is no right or wrong way of doing this; just explore your surroundings.

Other Ways to be Mindful

There are many other ways to be mindful. The goal of these exercises is to help you notice what you are doing in the present moment. This is a way you can feel calm and aware.

•Painting or drawing.

• Listening to music.

• Taking a shower.

• Watching the clouds in the sky.

(b)

Handout 3.2 (Continued)

Reviewing Compassion Process

Module 1: Dayroom fight, level drop, anger/anxiety, thinking loops; trick brain, "not my fault but my responsibility"

Module 2: Jordan's red circle scenario (anger); three circles, soothing rhythm-breathing

Now let's think of how to apply what we have been learning today to Jordan's situation. A few days after the dayroom fight, Jordan still thinks about his level being dropped. His attention is stuck on the past. When his attention is on his level, he stays angry. This is because our attention affects our emotions.

What have we learned in this module that might help Jordan?

Notes

Between-Session Practice

Let's try to apply what we have learned in in group so far. To start, think of a small life difficulty. Make sure you chose something small, like someone saying no to you, or losing a belonging. Try not to think about anything too extreme or heavy.

Let's begin by trying to get comfortable. Go ahead and sit upright, and gently close your eyes or, if you prefer, direct your gaze downward.

Now, bring to mind the small life difficulty that you have gone through recently. Let your body take the posture that it naturally takes when you are thinking about that negative event or disappointment. For example, a disappointed posture might have slumped shoulders.

Notice what emotions come up in you as you think about your challenge. (Pause.)

Notice how your body feels. Do you feel tense, anxious, angry, sad, etc.? (Pause.)

Notice what thoughts you have your negative event. (Pause.)

Now we're going to try to switch our attention as best we can. As you think of this negative event, I want you to gently move into a more compassionate body posture.

1. Sit with a straight back. Keep your head upright and your shoulders in line with your hips. Place your feet flat on the floor.
2. Lift your shoulders up and slightly backward.
3. Find a comfortable position for your hands that will not be distracting to you.
4. Breathe into your belly rather than your chest.
5. Bring a friendly facial expression to your body posture.
6. Keep your gaze fixed gently on a single spot on the floor or remain with your eyes closed if you feel comfortable.

Now let's try to activate our soothing system by doing soothing rhythm-breathing. Begin to slow and deepen your natural breath. Each time you breathe out, say internally in a friendly and supportive voice:

Body slowing down
Mind slowing down

As you find your rhythm, notice and focus on the feeling of inner slowing with each out breath. (Pause.)

Remember your intention to become more helpful, friendly, and compassionate. Along with this compassionate intention, remember that life is difficult. We all find ourselves here with a tricky brain that has been shaped by our genes and our life experiences. This is not our fault. This wisdom is part of compassion.

As we bring this practice to a close, connect with your body again. Feel your body in the chair in this moment. Slowly start to come back into the room, and open your eyes when you are ready.

Module 4

Feeling Safe and Receiving Compassion From Others

Aims:

- See how feeling safe is different from feeling under threat.
- Talk about why it is important to create an inner secure base.
- Use imagery to make a safe space.
- Talk about why we need compassion from others. Discuss why it can be hard to receive compassion from others.
- Create an ideal compassionate other.

DOI: 10.4324/9781003607564-5

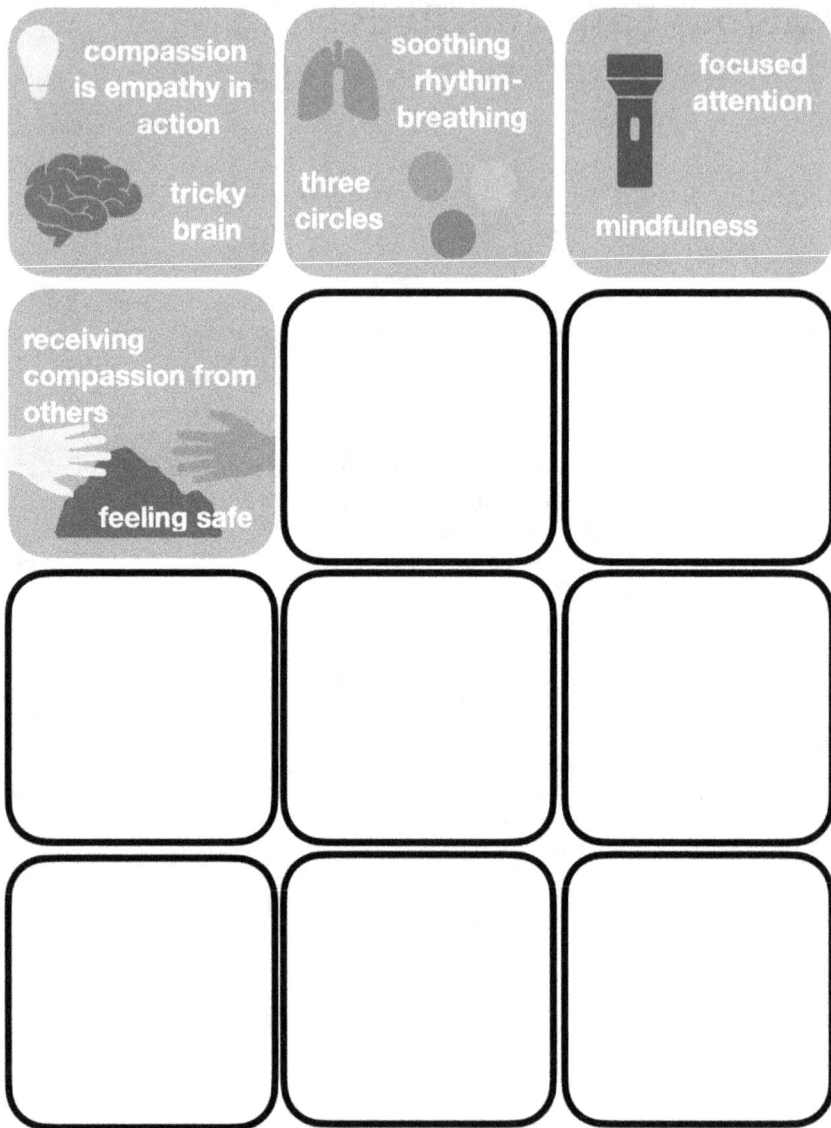

Figure 4 A visual representation of module 4 of 12.

Introduction

The last few modules have looked at how our brains, emotions, and past affect us. You'll remember that we have a set of emotions that help us deal with threats. We called this the red circle. We have talked about how many of us get caught in the threat system and spend little time in soothing. We want to find a balance between all of our emotion systems. In this module we will focus on wats to feel safe when threatened.

Feeling Threatened Versus Feeling Safe

When we feel threatened, we are looking to stop bad things from happening. The spotlight of our attention is on possible threats. This can be useful sometimes. On the other hand, when we feel safe, we can relax and enjoy our surroundings. When we feel safe, we take pleasure from where we are and begin to explore and try new things out. We can enjoy our life.

Turn to Handout 4.1 to look at the difference between feeling threatened and feeling safe.

Imagery

One way in which we can feel safer is through imagery. Imagery helps us to build our green circle. As we have seen before, our minds can have an impact on our bodies. This is why it helps to imagine feeling safe. Remember, this is our soothing system.

Some people worry that they will not be good at imagery. They may worry that they will not be able to create a clear picture in their mind. This is perfectly normal as we rarely have clear pictures in the mind. Images in our mind may not be very clear. Again, it's more important to try than to see it clearly. We aren't creating perfect photos in the mind. We are just imagining. What is most important.

Take some notes in Handout 4.2 and Handout 4.4 as we practice imagery together as a group. This will be useful as we continue practicing imagery of your safe place and ideal compassionate other.

Flows of Compassion

Now, let's talk about the flows of compassion. We can use these to feel safe. Take a look at the picture on Handout 4.3.

One flow is *compassion from others.*
Another flow is *compassion to others.*
Last, there is compassion for yourself, or *self-compassion.*

An easy way to remember this is that there are two flows: one flows in and one flows out. Self-compassion and compassion from others come into us. Compassion to others goes out from us to others. Each of these flows is important.

Receiving Compassion From Others

Let's focus on compassion from others. We need compassion from others. From the day we are born, we need other people. We need others to feed us, comfort us, and care for us to survive. This is the way that our brains are set up. Being cared for has the same importance as food.

Sadly, we sometimes don't get the care or attention we need. This can make us feel angry, anxious, sad, or distrusting. If we haven't gotten the compassion we needed in the past, our tricky brains can have a hard time accepting it later. In this case, receiving compassion is hard. Maybe, we avoid or reject compassion from others. This can happen when we are stuck in our threat system.

Again, this is not our fault, but it is our responsibility.

As we learn to accept compassion from others, we can feel more understood. We may also feel less lonely. Sometimes, we may think that we can only depend on ourselves. However, it can be helpful to start turning to others for support when we need it.

There is a practice at the end of this. It is called "Relating to the Image of Our Ideal Compassionate Other." You may recognize it from your group session. Feel free to focus on a practice that is most helpful to you.

Safety vs. Threat

FEELING
THREATENED

When we are focused on threat, we are looking to stop bad things from happening. This helps us survive, but constantly checking for threats can stop us from enjoying life.

Example: If a bird is constantly feeling threatened, it will fly away to stay safe, but it will have a hard time settling down to eat.

VS.

When we feel safe, we can explore our surroundings. We will have courage to even explore things we might fear or worry about. When we feel safe, we will also feel open to new experiences and will be able to grow.

Example: If a bird is able to feel safe, it will enjoy its food and will even have the freedom to build a nest.

FEELING SAFE

Handout 4.1 Safety Versus Threat

Your Safe Place

In the space below, write down features of your safe place.

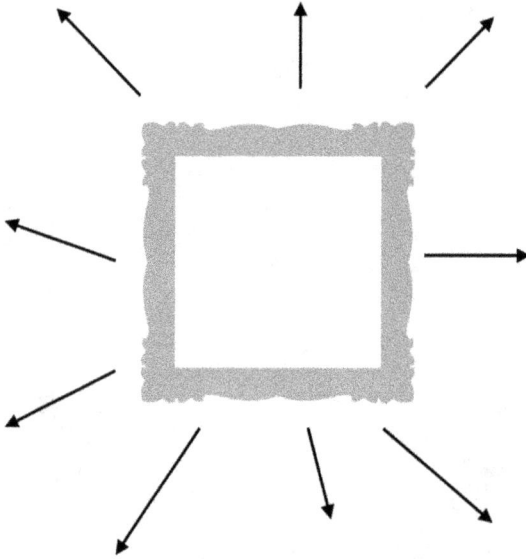

Handout 4.2 Your Safe Place

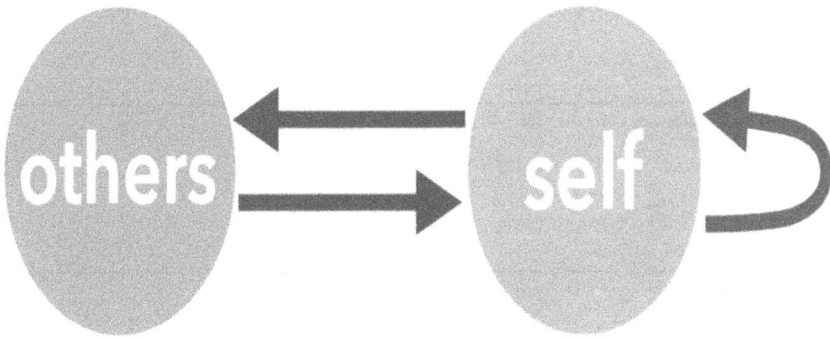

The Flows of Compassion

*Each flow is important. In this group we will be learning things we can do to increase each flow.

Handout 4.3 The Flows of Compassion

Building the Compassionate Image

Here you can write down everything you would want from a compassionate other.

How would you like your ideal compassionate caring image to appear? They can be a human, an animal, or anything else you would like.
How does your ideal compassionate other sound (e.g., the volume and texture of their voice)?
What other qualities would you like them to have (e.g., thoughtful, understanding, funny)?
How would you like this compassionate image to treat you?
How would you treat your compassionate image?

Handout 4.4 Building the Compassionate Image

Reviewing Compassion Process

Module 1: Dayroom fight, level drop, anger/anxiety, thinking loops; trick brain, "not my fault but my responsibility"

Module 2: Jordan's red circle scenario (anger); three circles, soothing rhythm-breathing

Module 3: Jordan's rumination on level drop, lingering anger; attention (flashlight), soothing rhythm-breathing

Now let's apply what we have been learning is this module to Jordan's situation. After Jordan's level was dropped, he worries he will get in trouble again. He finds himself focusing on potential threats. Any reactions from others make Jordan more upset than usual. After recognizing his emotions and realizing these worries are keeping him in the red circle, Jordan wants to feel safe.

What have we learned in this module that might help Jordan?

Notes

Between-Session Practice

Safe Place Imagery Exercise

Now, when you're ready, see if you can bring to mind a place where you feel okay and comfortable. This is ideally a place where you can feel safe and calm. This doesn't need to be somewhere you've been before or even a real place. Be creative, if you like, and see what you can imagine—somewhere that feels safe and comfortable.

If this is difficult for you, simply think of a type of place you would like to be in. Start simple. This may be a new experience for you. (Pause.)

Remember that there is no right or wrong way of doing this. This is just a way of exploring our minds a bit to see what happens. If possible, see if you can engage with a sense of curiosity and even playfulness. Allow yourself to see what emerges. (Pause.)

Think about the following: Would you prefer a place that is inside or outside? What is the weather like? Is it night or day? Is the air around you warm or cold?

Now consider some details of your safe place. Are you in a forest, or by the sea, or up a mountain, or near a nice garden? What is the light like? Is it dark or sunny?

If you're indoors, ask yourself, are you there because that allows you to feel comfortable? As much as you can, allow this safe place to be a place that you are not trying to escape anything. And, if you're indoors because you're trying to escape, afraid of what's outside, there's nothing wrong with that. For this imagery, however, you might want to consider somewhere that feels safe without trying to escape, whether that's indoors or out.

Next, imagine the kind of sounds that might be around you. What do you hear in your place? The wind softly pushing the grass? Waves crashing? Crickets chirping? (Pause.)

Imagine other sensations as well. What are you walking on? If you are barefoot in your safe place, how does the ground feel beneath your feet? What might you want to touch or hold? (Pause.)

Notice if you can smell anything in your safe space. If you could smell something in this place, what would you like to smell? Is it the freshness of the air, the spray of the ocean, or the sweetness of flowers? Just take a moment and notice. (Pause.)

Now we are going to imagine our relationship to our safe place. Though it may seem strange, we will imagine what it's like to experience this safe place welcoming us.

For a moment imagine that everything around you welcomes you. You have created this image in your mind so it's part of you. This place is connected to you.

Imagine that the place itself takes joy in you being here. For example, if there are clouds above you, they enjoy you being here. If there are trees around you, they take delight in you walking around seeing them. They make you feel welcomed. They make you feel that you belong.

Explore your feelings when you imagine this place is happy with you being there. Create a friendly and open facial expression as you imagine being welcomed. Allow yourself to have a soft smile of pleasure at being there. Remember the friendly voice tone that we practiced last week. (Pause.)

You may notice that as you think about doing things in your safe place, the place may change around you. This is normal and commonly happens. You don't have to hold onto only one image of this place if your mind wants it to change. Again, the idea is to allow your mind to explore because you feel safe. (Pause.)

Now slowly start letting that image fade, come back into the room, and notice how your body feels in your chair. When you are ready, open your eyes.

Building an "Ideal Compassionate Other" Imagery Exercise

Go ahead and gently close your eyes or cast your gaze to the ground. We're going to start to imagine our ideal compassionate other. This compassionate other is wise, kind, helpful, insightful, and so on.

Ideal means that the compassionate other doesn't have to suffer from human fallibility, weakness, or bad habits. It is exactly what you would want, even if it's unrealistic. The act of creating this other is what is important for how our minds work.

Maybe start by thinking about appearance. As I said before, sometimes people prefer not to think about humans but may think of an animal or an object. The key to creating this compassionate other is that it has its own mind that completely it understands what you are going through. It understands that we have tricky brains and that we can suffer and get caught in loops with our own minds. See what emerges for you. Just take a moment to consider the following:

- Would you want your ideal compassionate other to have a gender? If so, what gender would you prefer? (Pause.)
- What is the age of your ideal compassionate other? Older? Younger? The same age? (Pause.)
- What sort of size would this ideal compassionate other be? (Pause.)
- Do you have any sense of facial expressions? (Pause.)
- Do you have an impression of hair color or eye color if they have hair or eyes? Remember, you don't need to see anything clearly; just have an impression. (Pause.)
- How might they be clothed? (Pause.)

Next, we can start to think about how they communicate with you:

- What sort of voice tone or sounds would you like for this compassionate other to have? Again, you do not need to have a clear picture of this. Allow a sense of this to be enough. (Pause.)

There are many qualities you may want for your compassionate other. You may want your compassionate other to be patient. You may want them to be tolerant, wise, and friendly. Perhaps your compassionate other is gentle, open, and understanding. You can want a compassionate other with strength, determination, playfulness, and humor. Many people want a compassionate other that is easy to be with. Of course, there may be other qualities that you would like as well. Think of the qualities you would like yours to have. (Pause.)

Try to turn this image into one that you would like to be with and feel safe with. If you don't feel comfortable with the image, then play around with it. Play with it until it has the qualities you'd like so that you are comfortable with it.

Sometimes people want their image to have been through what they've been through and have wisdom and understanding from that. For example, a person who has dealt with depression may prefer a compassionate other that has dealt with depression like them. Therefore, this compassionate other understands them. It has wise and supportive advice. Your ideal compassionate other is close to you. It is understanding and shares wisdom with you; it knows who you are and what you've been through. Your compassionate other wants to address your suffering and help in any way it can. The ideal compassionate other certainly does not cause suffering in any way. Take a moment to really think about your compassionate other. Think of the characteristics it has. (Pause.)

Now, just slowly let that image fade away. Notice how your body feels in the chair right now, and when you are ready, open your eyes.

The Compassionate Self

Aims:

- Introduce, define, and practice self-compassion.
- Explore challenges and difficulties related to self-compassion.
- Begin to develop a sense of your own compassionate self.

DOI: 10.4324/9781003607564-6

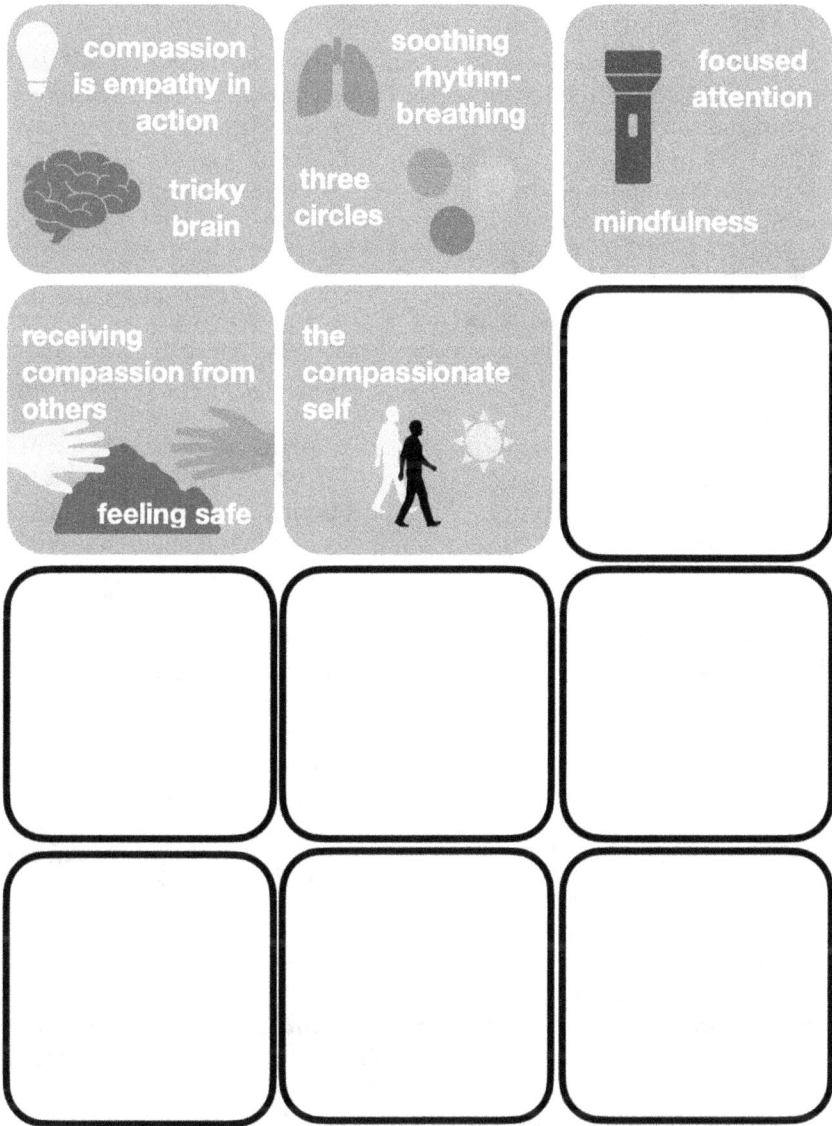

Figure 5 A visual representation of module 5 of 12.

Introduction

The focus of this module will be on building our compassionate self. Remember our definition of compassion. Compassion is having a sensitivity to pain and suffering in self and others with a commitment to try to relieve and prevent it. In summary, compassion is both doing good and avoiding harm. This also applies to being compassionate toward *yourself*.

The Compassionate Self

Let's explore your compassionate self. Think of a time when you wanted to help someone who was struggling. What were you paying attention to? What were you thinking? How did it feel in your body? How did you want to act? This exercise shows that you already have some idea about what it means to be compassionate. You can use this wisdom to develop a compassionate self.

Compassion is like a muscle. We are all born with and have it, but it gets stronger and serves us better when we exercise. You might also think of compassion like riding a bike, in the beginning it is hard but eventually with practice it becomes easy.

Think back on our first few sessions when we talked about how we didn't choose all of our environment or the body we were born into. If we had been born into a very different environment, we may be very different people. Consider how you act differently throughout the day based on your changing environment. Think about all of the emotions you've had over the last week. Was there a time, even a brief time, when you felt happy? Anxious? Sad? Scared? Peaceful? Our state of being is constantly changing.

Although outside factors can influence our emotional state, we can intentionally move the flashlight of our attention to focus on things that will help us to develop a more compassionate state. Focusing on things that make us feel compassionate, kind, and joyful can help us to develop this more compassionate mind. Remember our previous mindfulness practices where we moved the flashlight of our attention. We can move this flashlight whenever we want to help us focus on things that make us more compassionate.

Start to think of what your compassionate self would look like, try to step into it. This about these questions: What does it feel like a compassionate person? What kind of thoughts do you have? What kind of behaviors? What desires do you have? It might be helpful to think of someone you know who is compassionate. Imagine what it would be like to become like that person. Then try to see the world through that person's eyes. Just try to experiment with this and notice what it's like.

Turn to Handout 5.1 to write down some qualities of your compassionate self. Next, Handout 5.2a and 5.2b will help you explore just how different your threatened self is from your compassionate self.

The Compassionate Self

In the space below, write down qualities of your
compassionate self

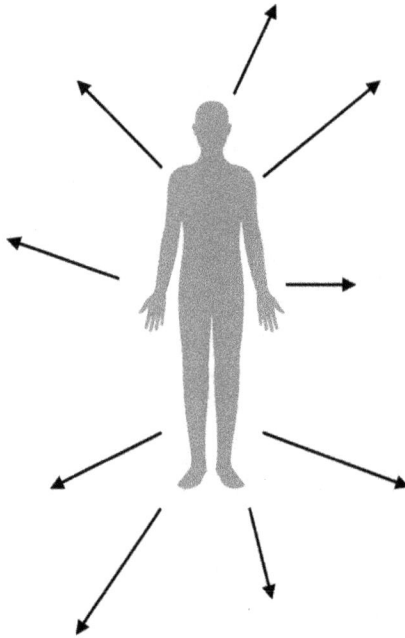

Handout 5.1 The Compassionate Self

A "Red Circle" Self Response

Think about a difficult situation, but nothing that causes too much distress.
As best as you can, think about how your "red-circle" self would react. After, we will
compared the response to your compassionate-self.

My "red-circle" self thinks:

_____

_____

_____

_____

My "red-circle" self does:

_____

_____

_____

_____

How I feel (as my "red-circle" self):

_____

_____

_____

_____

Handout 5.2A A "Red Circle" Self Response

A Compassionate Self Response

Think about a difficult situation, but nothing that causes too much distress.
As best as you can, think about how your compassionate-self would react. Notice
how different this response is compared to your "red-circle" self.

My "compassionate self" thinks:

_____

_____

_____

_____

My "compassionate self" does:

_____

_____

_____

_____

How I feel (as my "compassionate self"):

_____

_____

_____

_____

Handout 5.2B A Compassionate Self Response

Reviewing Compassion Process

Module 1: Dayroom fight, level drop, anger/anxiety, thinking loops; trick brain, "not my fault but my responsibility"

Module 2: Jordan's red circle scenario (anger); three circles, soothing rhythm-breathing

Module 3: Jordan's rumination on level drop, lingering anger; attention (flashlight), soothing rhythm-breathing

Module 4: Jordan's continuing threat mode; feelings safe through secure place/compassionate other imagery

Now let's apply what we have learned in this module to Jordan's situation. Like us, Jordan already has some understanding of what compassion is. He can use that understanding to purposefully be compassionate. He wants to activate his compassionate self.

What have we learned in this module that might help Jordan?

Notes

Between-Session Practice

Activating the Compassionate Self Exercise

Let's start with grounding ourselves and getting into a physical state that more easily allows for compassion. Try to notice:

- Feeling grounded; feeling heavier in the chair; sitting firm and stable, like a mountain
- Compassionate breathing that's slower and more open
- Compassionate posture, with shoulders back and back straight, relaxed but alert
- Compassionate facial expression and inner voice

Remember, if you find yourself being distracted from these things, or my voice, shine your flashlight back on them. This is mindfulness. If you feel comfortable doing so, you can close your eyes.

Now take a moment and try to step into your compassionate self.
What does it feel like to be that kind of compassionate person?
What kind of thoughts do you have?
What kind of behaviors?
What desires do you have?

Take a moment to really imagine what it would be like to be this compassionate self. If you notice that you're having difficulty, just notice this difficulty, and then gently bring your attention back to what it would be like to be your perfectly compassionate self. See if you can feel it in your mind and your body. When you are ready, you may open your eyes.

Now attend to the compassionate quality of wisdom—we have the wisdom that all of us have a tricky brain that we didn't choose. At times it can be chaotic, tricky, and painful—and this isn't our fault. This wisdom helps us understand ourselves and others.

We also have the wisdom of how we've dealt with things in our life, and we have wisdom from natural compassion for those we care about that need help.

Let's imagine waking up in the morning. What would it look like to have compassionate wisdom?

Now attend to the compassionate quality of strength. As you ground yourself with your breathing, notice your sense of groundedness and strength. Notice how that feels in your body and your mind. You have the ability to feel stronger and more grounded.

Let's imagine eating a meal. What would it look like to have compassionate strength?

Now attend to the compassionate quality of commitment. See if you can feel committed to be compassionate; do you wish to be somebody who is helpful to others and who would not carelessly or purposely harm them? Do you wish to be helpful to yourself, and to not carelessly or purposely harm yourself?

Let's imagine meeting someone new. What would it look like to have compassionate commitment?

Notice how good it feels to be centered in this compassionate self. Try to picture what it would feel and look like in other scenarios if you could be like this. What would it look or feel like to sit or stand? What voice tones or facial expressions would there be? See if you can focus on your commitment to try being this way. Hold this in your mind for a few moments on your own. (Pause.)

Now bring to mind someone that you care deeply about. Try to focus on that person and notice what wishes you have for them. Now take a moment to think of someone you've only briefly crossed paths with. Try to focus on this person for a moment. See if you can feel compassion toward them as well. Can you wish them well? Think about how you feel. (Pause.)

When you feel ready, come back to the room.

The Nature of Multiple Emotions and Finding Balance

Aims:

- Learn about experiencing multiple emotions at once, specifically threat emotions (anger, fear, and sadness).
- Learn how different emotions affect your thoughts, behaviors, and memories, and learn specific ways of settling for specific emotions.
- Discuss how the compassionate self can allow us to balance different emotions.

DOI: 10.4324/9781003607564-7

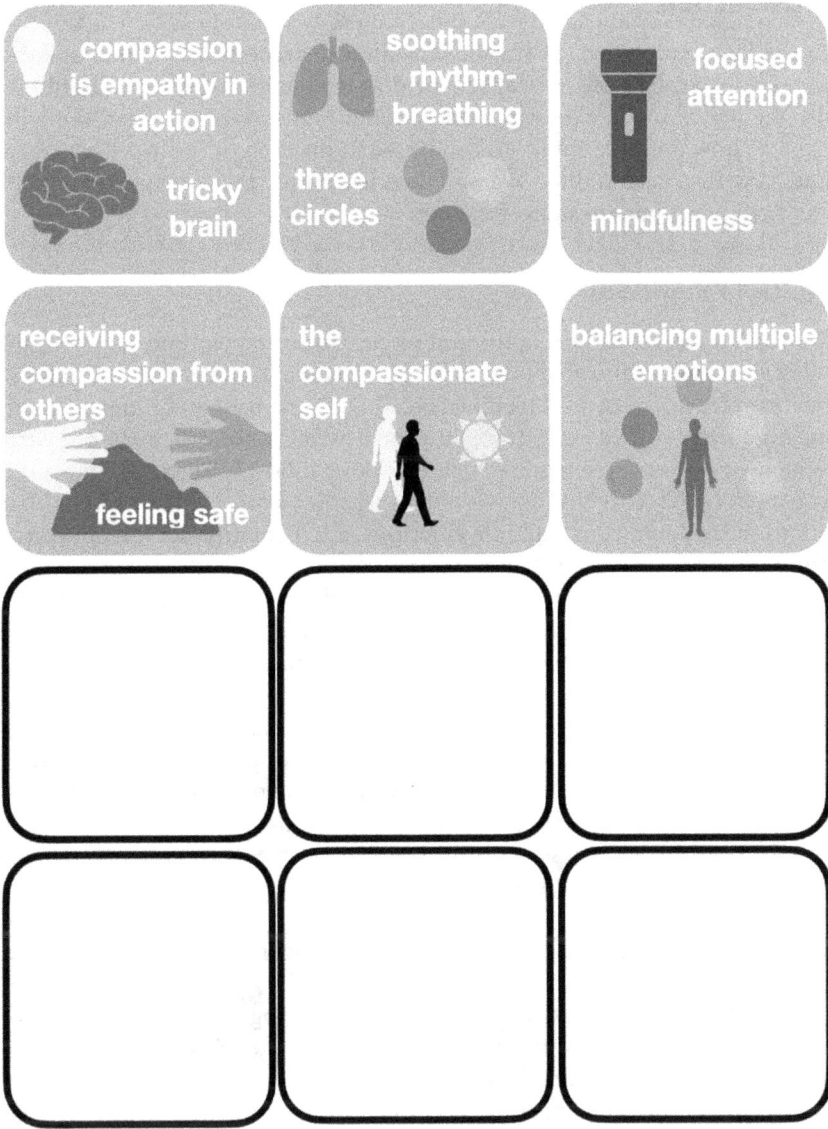

Figure 6 A visual representation of module 6 of 12.

Introduction

In the last module we spent time working to strengthen the compassionate self. Next, let's see how specific emotions might make things hard for us. We will start by exploring different emotions, one at a time. We will explore how multiple emotions can be felt at once, emotions work together and how they can conflict. We will then learn how the compassionate self can help bring our emotions together.

Multiple Emotions

We can all feel multiple emotions at once. For example, think of an argument you had with somebody. This could be an argument with a family member, friend, peer, staff member, etc. Take a moment and bring to mind an argument you've had. Start to think: What emotions were present? Which emotions came first? Which emotions follow? Which emotions do you prefer? Which emotions would you rather avoid? Turn to Handout 6.1 to write down your multiple emotions. Each emotion serves a purpose and has its own desire and motivation.

Though we have many emotions, we're going to look at the three major threat emotions in this module. Then we will talk about how our compassionate self can help us with these threat emotions.

- The first is anger. Anger is linked to a sense of having been wronged or attacked. The motivation or drive is typically to protect or attack back.
- The next is fear. Fear is linked to threat and being vulnerable. It is motivated to prevent or avoid things that worry us.
- Finally, there is sadness, which is linked to loss. Sadness is motivated to tell us that something is wrong.

These three emotions are usually involved the most in mental health struggles.

Now let's explore these big three emotions. Bring to mind again the argument we talked about earlier. Let's start with anger. Allow your mind to go over what was said and how you felt angry. Let's see if we can explore the different aspects of anger by going through the questions below. As you do, fill out Handout 6.2.

Motives: What has triggered your anger? What do you want when you're angry? What would be a good outcome for anger? What is the function or the point and purpose of your anger? What do we feel would happen if we didn't have anger or express anger?

Thoughts: What are the thoughts that are going through your mind when you are angry?

Body states: What happens in your body when the angry pattern turns up? Where is your feeling in your body? What is your facial expression like? What is your voice tone like? What is your body posture when angry? If your anger was to build and build, how would that be? Where would it go in your body?

Behaviors: What does anger want you to do? If anger was in complete control and didn't care about the consequences, what would you do?

Memories: What does the anger make you remember when reflecting on conflicts with others? What memories come to you when you are angry? What are the memories that you associate with feeling angry that are particularly powerful or important for you? How far do they go back in time? To childhood?

Settling: How do you cope with anger? How do you settle when you're angry?

We will move through the same process next for anxiety and then sadness if we have time.

Bringing in the Compassionate Self

Compassion plays an important role by bringing all these emotions together. It brings together anger, anxiety, and sadness. The compassionate self helps you to see the role of each emotion. Further, compassion helps you shift out of the threat system and into the caring motivation system. Compassion uses compassion uses wisdom, strength, and commitment. It uses those qualities to deal with these various emotions that at times are in conflict.

Let's explore the compassionate self by first finishing Handout 6.2. We will consider the motives, thoughts, body states, behaviors, and memories, as well as ways we grow as our compassionate self. Notice how different the compassionate self is from our threat emotions.

Last, turn to Handout 6.3 as we explore how our compassionate self views our anger, fear, and sadness.

Exploring Multiple Emotions

Think about a difficult situation, but nothing too distressing. Try to write all of the possible emotions that arise regarding the situation.

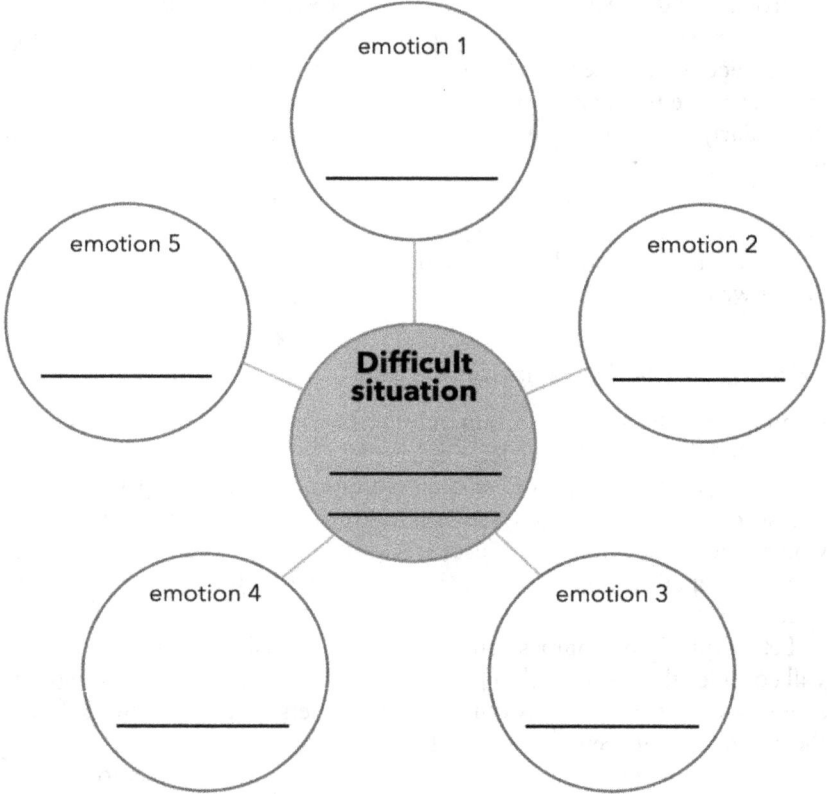

emotion 1

_____

emotion 5

_____

Difficult situation

_____

_____

emotion 2

_____

emotion 4

_____

emotion 3

_____

Handout 6.1 Exploring Multiple Emotions

Exploring Multiple Emotions in Detail

Anger	Fear
Motives:	*Motives:*
Thoughts:	*Thoughts:*
Body:	*Body:*
Behavior:	*Behavior:*
Memories:	*Memories:*
Settle:	*Settle:*
Sadness	**Compassionate-Self**
Motives:	*Motives:*
Thoughts:	*Thoughts:*
Body:	*Body:*
Behavior:	*Behavior:*
Memories:	*Memories:*
Settle:	*Growth:*

Handout 6.2 Exploring Multiple Emotions in Detail

Compassionate View of Threat Emotions

→ **ANGER**

How might your compassionate-self view your anger?

_____

_____

_____

→ **FEAR**

How might your compassionate-self view your fear?

_____

_____

_____

→ **SADNESS**

How might your compassionate-self view your sadness?

_____

_____

_____

Handout 6.3 Compassionate View of Threat Emotions

Reviewing Compassion Process

Module 1: Dayroom fight, level drop, anger/anxiety, thinking loops; trick brain, "not my fault but my responsibility"

Module 2: Jordan's red circle scenario (anger); three circles, soothing rhythm-breathing

Module 3: Jordan's rumination on level drop, lingering anger; attention (flashlight), soothing rhythm-breathing

Module 4: Jordan's continuing threat mode; feelings safe through secure place/compassionate other imagery

Module 5: Jordan intentionally shifts to compassion; self-compassion in action (wisdom, strength, commitment)

Now let's apply what we have learned today to Jordan's situation. Jordan felt many emotions when his level was dropped. He was angry with the staff, sad to be farther from discharge, and anxious he might get into trouble again. These are all red circle emotions, or threat emotions. These emotions want him to do different things. His anger makes him want to yell at staff. His sadness makes him want to cry. His anxiety makes him want to stay in his room. With all these emotions, Jordan is feeling overwhelmed.

What have we learned in this module that might help Jordan?

Notes

Between-Session Practice

Compassionate Self for Emotional Growth Regulation and Integration

We've learned that we have different emotions that arise when we have problems and conflicts. These are usually threat emotions and they can be quite intense. Threat emotions can pull us in a number of different directions. Often, we don't want any one of the threat emotions to run the show because, while they all have potential benefits, they also have significant drawbacks. So we need to tune in and find a part of ourselves that has the courage and wisdom to act in a way that we want. Using just anger or just fear may not be the wisest or most helpful approach in managing conflict or other problems.

You can probably guess which part of ourselves we are going to try to access and see how this part thinks and wants to act—our compassionate self!

First, we need to activate our compassionate self. Sit with your shoulders back, spine straight, and chest open. Remember your friendly facial expression and friendly inner voice tone as we do this exercise. Please close your eyes if you feel comfortable doing so.

Now bring your attention to your breathing. Connect with your soothing rhythm-breathing. Notice the sensation of your mind slowing down, then your body slowing down. Become more grounded and stable in the body. Remember your friendly facial expression and friendly voice tone.

So, remember your wisdom that we all happen to find ourselves here as a part of the flow of life, with our tricky brains. We didn't design the brains that we have that give rise to all kinds of emotions from our threat system. Nor did we choose the environments we grew up in that shaped us for good and perhaps not so good. Therefore, so much has happened that is not our fault. But it is our responsibility to try as best we can to cultivate the help within us. And this is what compassion does.

So compassionate wisdom is understanding that we have all just arrived here with a difficult brain and life circumstances that give rise to suffering, and that is not our fault. We didn't choose this situation, and we may not want it. The question then becomes, how might we deal with it?

The second key quality is inner strength. And that comes partly from wisdom of understanding the nature of life and the flow of life. We all find ourselves here trying to do our best. And it also comes from our posture, breathing, and grounding. These all contribute to our strength as we become stable as a mountain. So, compassion is wise, and it has a sense of strength. It is not weak.

The third quality is commitment. Because of our wisdom, we know that we are all caught up in the cycle of life. Because of our strength, we engage with suffering as a part of the flow of life. And because of our commitment, we try to be as helpful, supportive, and kind as we can be when we encounter suffering, whether it be in ourselves or others. By slowing down, connecting with the breath, and grounding the body, we can reconnect with the compassionate qualities of strength, wisdom, and commitment.

Slowly come back into the room.

Self-Criticism

Aims:

- Learn about why we monitor ourselves.
- See how monitoring can lead to self-criticism.
- Explore what it would feel like to let go of self-criticism.
- Explore compassion as another way to help us work on our goals compared to using self-criticism.

DOI: 10.4324/9781003607564-8

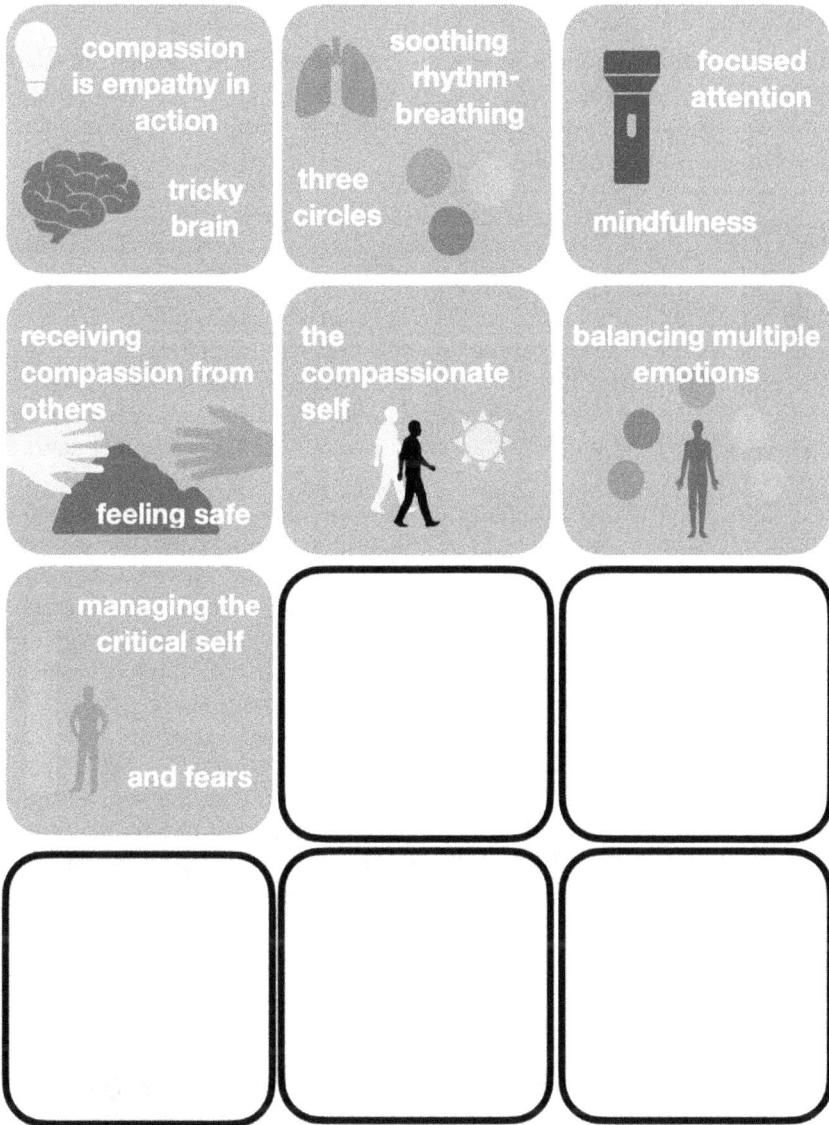

Figure 7 A visual representation of module 7 of 12.

Introduction

The focus of this module is self-criticism. We will be looking at what self-criticism is and what it can do to us. We will explore what kinds of things make us feel self-criticism. Then we will see how we can instead respond to those things with compassion.

Self-Monitoring

First, let's think about how and why we monitor ourselves. Let's start by thinking about a smoke alarm. What is a smoke alarm doing? Before it goes off, what is it doing? Many systems that we use in everyday life are constantly monitoring how they are working. For example, smoke alarms are detecting for smoke and then sounding an alarm. Systems monitor themselves because they have a function—to keep the system operating properly and efficiently.

Brains are essentially monitoring systems. It is monitoring you and your body in many ways. Inside of you, a monitoring system is always at work. We can monitor and then make judgments for all sorts of things, from memories to emotional states. For example, you might be monitoring what's happening in our group today, how therapy is going, how you're getting along with other group members, or whether you think other people are doing better than you. This is the way our brains operate. So we can begin to look at a variety of monitoring patterns we engage in.

Along with this monitoring system comes an expectation or an idea-self. For example, when you're at work, you are presenting yourself in a way you feel good about. A lot of times, our actual self doesn't align perfectly with our ideal self. This difference between the two can be referred to as the "disappointment gap." When this happens, we might attack ourselves for our shortcomings. A name that we have for these kinds of attacks is self-criticism.

Self-Criticism

We want to protect ourselves from danger or negative outcomes in life, so we try to use self-criticism to fix the things that we think are wrong with ourselves. For example, let's say that you were thinking that you would be discharged soon and were really excited about it, then you weren't discharged after all. You might start thinking about what you are doing wrong, and have thoughts like "I'm so stupid. If I was better at participating in therapy, then maybe I wouldn't be here anymore." Thoughts like these may feel safe because they seem to motivate us to do better, which can help us move toward our goals. However, thoughts like these put us in the red circle (or the threat system) and actually make us feel worse.

Imagine we could take away your self-criticism so that you'd never get angry with or beat yourself up in the future. What would be your greatest fears? What would you worry about if you didn't have your self-criticism anymore?

Some may fear that they would become lazy. Others may fear that they would not learn from their mistakes. Some may worry that they would not even notice their mistakes. We often think that our critical voice is there to help us. This part of us that is self-critical may have useful goals. When we look more deeply, though, we can see it often makes us feel worse.

Let's explore your critical self by filing out Handout 7.1.

Using the Compassionate Self

We can decrease our self-critic by learning to fail compassionately. This is the ability to be disappointed, imperfect, and fall short of our ideals without launching attacks on ourselves. We want to improve, of course, not by self-attacking but by having self-compassion.

Once we know how to deal compassionately with ourselves when things go wrong, we're not frightened of mistakes or failure. Then we're free to develop confidence and strengthen our skills. But if we always monitor ourselves and are frightened about making mistakes, then we will constantly be putting ourselves down, which makes life more difficult.

Imagine you have a child you love, and you have a choice of two schools. As you walk through the gates to one of the schools you see a group of teachers who look a lot like your self-critics. They say that they will ensure your child learns because if your child makes mistakes, or is lazy, or is arrogant in some way, they will be critical and harsh. They will express their anger and contempt. They will ensure strong discipline and instill the fear of authority through punishment. So you thank them very much, and then you walk to the other school, which is a school filled with compassionate education. Which school do you want? The compassionate school would help you child more in the long run.

Let's turn to Handout 7.2 to look at how different our compassionate self is from our critical-self.

Functional Analysis - Self-Criticism

Greatest fears:			
Looks like:	Says to me:	Feels about me:	Does to me:
What I am now thinking and feeling about myself:			

Handout 7.1A Functional Analysis of Self-Criticism

Functional Analysis - Self-Criticism
Worked Example

Greatest fears:

Become arrogant; hurt other people; go wild; never get anything done; embarrass myself; be lazy; be criticized by others; have no friends.

Looks like:	Says to me:	Feels about me:	Does to me:
Angry self; monster with big mouth and sharp teeth, a greenish slimy thing, black eyes, a big shadow; pointing finger.	You're pathetic; you always are a disappointment; you are a screw up; you aren't good; you're a coward; you're disgusting; if people really knew about you, they wouldn't like you.	Anger; disappointment; disgust; shame; rejection.	Shut me up; kick me; shake me to wake up; shout; give up on me.

What I am now thinking and feeling about myself:

Sadness; loneliness; anger; tiredness; exhausted; betrayed; depressed.

Handout 7.1B Functional Analysis of Self-Criticism (Worked Example)

Functional Analysis - Compassionate-Self

Greatest wishes for me:			
Looks like:	Says to me:	Feels about me:	Does to/for me:
What I am now thinking and feeling about myself:			

Handout 7.2A Functional Analysis of the Compassionate Self

Functional Analysis : Compassionate-Self

Worked Example

Greatest wishes for me:
Be less selfish; be true to myself; feel safe; be kind to myself and others; live a valued life; be humble; be helpful; have courage; keep going if it gets tough.

Looks like:	Says to me:	Feels about me:	Does to/for me:
Mother Earth; butterfly; angel; sunflower; sun.	Life is tricky; it's not your fault; let's see what we can do; it is okay; you are okay; this is disappointing but we can try again; you have a good heart.	Unconditional love; care; acceptance; connected; committed; trusting.	Be a support; just be there; hold my hand; act like a friend.

What I am now thinking and feeling about myself:
Light; hopeful; soothed; not judged; energized; accepted.

Handout 7.2B Functional Analysis of the Compassionate Self (Worked Example)

Reviewing Compassion Process

Module 1: Dayroom fight, level drop, anger/anxiety, thinking loops; trick brain, "not my fault but my responsibility"

Module 2: Jordan's red circle scenario (anger); three circles, soothing rhythm-breathing

Module 3: Jordan's rumination on level drop, lingering anger; attention (flashlight), soothing rhythm-breathing

Module 4: Jordan's continuing threat mode; feelings safe through secure place/compassionate other imagery

Module 5: Jordan intentionally shifts to compassion; self-compassion in action (wisdom, strength, commitment)

Module 6: Jordan's dayroom situation produces multiple emotions; compassionate self understands and balances emotions

Let's see how Jordan experienced the inner critic. When Jordan's level was dropped, he experienced self-critical thoughts. Jordan thinks about how he should have been able to show that the fight was not his fault. He thinks, "If I was better about explaining myself and proving that I didn't start the fight, I wouldn't have gotten in trouble. But because I am not good at communicating with others, I was blamed for something I didn't do. It's my fault. I'm so stupid." These self-critical thoughts are not helpful, and they make Jordan feel worse about himself. When Jordan listens to these thoughts, they add to his anger, sadness, and other negative emotions.

What have we learned in this module that might help Jordan?

Notes

Between-Session Practice

This exercise is meant to help us explore our self-critic. It helps us see that the self-critic is not kind to us. It does not have our best interests at heart.

Compassion Takes the Lead

Take a moment to check your posture. Place your feet flat on the floor and open your back into an upright position. Slow your breathing for just a minute. Let's start to work with that pattern of ourselves that monitors us in a rather critical and sometimes hurtful way. See if the compassionate part and pattern within you can help it. First, we are giving space to engage our compassionate self. Slowing the breathing a little, centering our awareness in the body, feeling grounded. Noticing that we have our strength and wisdom and commitment to do this work.

Now imagine your critical self in front of you, being critical. You are watching it. Hold to your compassionate position, be your compassionate self. Now as you are observing the critical piece being critical, see if you can look behind the critic and see what's driving it. Can you see any fears? Rejection? Inferiority? Not being wanted? Consider the pains that brought that fear to life, such as disappointments or what people may have said. Why is this self-criticism so harsh? Could it be sadness? Loss? What's behind this harsh attitude? Imagine your compassionate self is curious about the needs and fears of this self-critical part of you.

Holding our compassionate position, we now offer a compassionate wish. We wish that whatever is causing this desire to be critical may stop. We wish to find peace.

What compassionate message would you like to leave the critical self with? As your compassionate self, ask yourself these questions: What would you like to hear and to know? What would you need to feel peace?

You might offer messages to your critic, such as:

- I see you are frustrated and tired. However, the way you are trying to motivate me is not working. You can rest. I'm doing this job; I'm taking the lead. Thank you for trying.
- I know you are scared or angry, but you can feel safe now. I'm leading the change; everything will be smoother for all of us.
- May you feel safe and at peace.

Slowly bring your attention back to the room as you are ready. Notice sounds; notice your body. Open your eyes.

Module 8

Shame and Guilt

Aims:

- Explore how the threat, drive, and soothing systems are influenced by our social relationships.
- Learn how our threat system is geared for self-monitoring.
- Learn about the differences between shame and guilt.
- Explore how tuning into one's compassionate self can help heal shame and, when appropriate, shift to guilt.

DOI: 10.4324/9781003607564-9

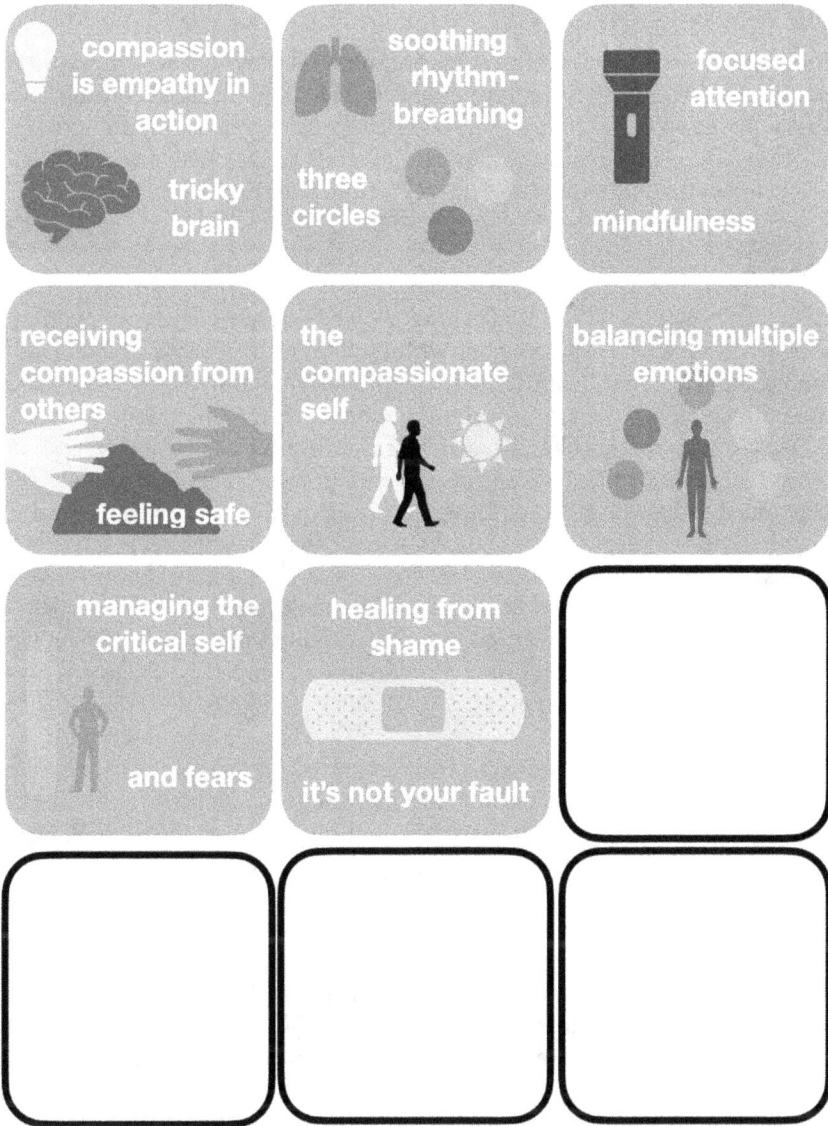

Figure 8 A visual representation of module 8 of 12.

Introduction

In the last module we looked at self-criticism. In this module we will explore another set of emotions that are connected to self-criticism. We call these shame-based emotions. These emotions lead us to feel bad and can hurt our relationships. These emotions can lead us to be stuck in the threat system. We will see how the compassionate self can help us deal with shame.

Shame

Let's first explore how our brains have evolved. Have you seen any wildlife shows on TV where animals fight with each other over resources? For example, animals often fight over access to the best hunting spots or watering holes. Imagine two lions approaching a watering hole. What might happen?

We also face threats like animals. We can withdraw or become aggressive when facing social threat. Some people tend to be anxious and submissive, frightened of being criticized. Others are very quick to become aggressive. So what we experience when we face social threats is affected by how our brains are built. Shame and similar emotions are related to things we feel about ourselves if we think other people do not approve of us.

Shame is an important self-conscious emotion to understand. When we feel shame, we usually feel it in a global sense of ourselves. There are two parts to shame.

- With external shame, our attention and our focus go outward. We worry about what others think and feel about us.
- With internal shame, our attention and our focus go inward. We are focused on what we think and feel about ourselves.

Turn to Handout 8.1 to review the difference between internal and external shame. Write down what happens in your body when you feel shame.

Let's explore shame more closely by turning to Handout 8.2. Look at what you feel when you imagine sharing something shameful with others. Remember, we often feel multiple emotions at once. Then think what you fear when feeling shame and what you do when you feel think way. Start thinking about how shame has impacted your life.

Guilt

Another self-conscious emotion is guilt. It is often confused with shame, but they are actually quite different. Guilt is the regret we feel when we have caused harm. Guilt evolved from the caring system. When mammals evolved caring behavior, they also had to evolve ways of detecting and avoiding harm to those they cared for. It turns out guilt is linked to this harm avoidance. Guilt inspires us to try to repair harm if we cause it. With guilt, we are not worried about whether people look down on us or like us. We are not concerned about defending ourselves. Guilt makes us feel a desire to improve.

Shame Versus Guilt

Note how shame is different from guilt. Shame tends to be much more self-focused. If we have been harmful and try to repair that harm out of shame, we try to help ourselves feel better. We want the other person to forgive us and like us again. In contrast, guilt is behavior-focused. Guilt requires empathy, whereas shame does not.

There is a lot of evidence now that if we can tolerate feeling guilt, then we are able to feel a sense of responsibility and behave morally and in caring and compassionate ways. It is very important that we learn to tolerate guilt without attacking ourselves, without feeling shame.

Imagine that two kids (we'll call them Ty and Isaiah) have both stolen candy from the store and been caught. Ty feels shame because he automatically thinks, "Oh, people will not like me now, and my parents will be angry and not love me!" He is focusing on what others think about him. He might also feel bad about himself (e.g., "I'm a bad person to have done this"). All of his focus is on himself. This is called shame. Isaiah, on the other hand, does not focus on himself but on the harm that he has done, with a great sense of remorse and sorrow for the pain he has caused. His genuine wish is to try to repair or make amends for his actions. His attention is not on himself but on the harm he has done. This is called guilt.

From this example, we can see that guilt is very important for us because when we allow ourselves to feel to guilt, we are open to recognizing any harm that we have caused other people. This allows us to take responsibility and turn our focus to putting things right, if we can. Remember, in compassion focused therapy, our intention is to try to address suffering. Guilt can help us do this.

Turn to Handout 8.3; filling this out will help us to explore the difference between shame and guilt. In this group, we hope to shift from shame to guilt so we can heal from shame.

Internal vs. External Shame

External Shame:

- Our attention is on what other people are thinking
- It is normal; all of us care about how others view us
- Fear of disapproval, social rejection, and isolation
- Makes it difficult to be open with our thoughts and emotions

Shame is a bodily experience. What happens in your body when you feel shame?

Internal Shame:

- Our attention is inwards, on ourselves
- Self-criticism
- Underneath is the fear of external shame

Handout 8.1 Internal Versus External Shame

Exploring Shame

What feelings come up for me when I think I might have to share something shameful?		
How do I think other people would react and treat me if they knew?	In the moment, how do I react when I feel shame?	How do I usually cope when I feel shame?
How has shame influenced my life?		

Handout 8.2 Exploring Shame

Shame vs. Guilt

For the situations below, write a shame- and guilt-based responses to each. Think about which you would be most helpful.

Imagine that you lose your temper with a child, and you shout at them.

Shame response: _____

Guilt response: _____

Imagine that you forget your friend's birthday, and they call you up to remind you.

Shame response: _____

Guilt response: _____

Imagine that because life has been difficult, you turn to drugs, and that has negative consequences.

Shame response: _____

Guilt response: _____

Think of how your compassionate-self could help you in each situation.

Handout 8.3 Shame Versus Guilt

Reviewing Compassion Process

Module 1: Dayroom fight, level drop, anger/anxiety, thinking loops; trick brain, "not my fault but my responsibility"

Module 2: Jordan's red circle scenario (anger); three circles, soothing rhythm-breathing

Module 3: Jordan's rumination on level drop, lingering anger; attention (flashlight), soothing rhythm-breathing

Module 4: Jordan's continuing threat mode; feelings safe through secure place/compassionate other imagery

Module 5: Jordan intentionally shifts to compassion; self-compassion in action (wisdom, strength, commitment)

Module 6: Jordan's dayroom situation produces multiple emotions; compassionate self understands and balances emotions

Module 7: Jordan's self-criticism; understanding inner critic and turning to growth through compassion

Let's see how Jordan deals with shame. After finding out his level had been dropped, Jordan yelled at the staff. He blamed them for keeping him from being discharged. After a while, Jordan feels embarrassed about losing his temper. He thinks, "Now the staff will think I'm immature for yelling. They won't like me anymore. What if the other patients heard and now think bad things about me too? That would be so embarrassing." Here, Jordan is feeling shame. He worries that others are thinking bad things about him.

What have we learned in this module that might help Jordan?

Notes

Between-Session Practice

Compassionate Intention

We prepare to develop our compassionate intention:

1. Sit with a straight back. Keep your head upright and your shoulders in line with your hips. Place your feet flat on the floor.
2. Lift your shoulders up and slightly backward.
3. Find a comfortable position for your hands that will not be distracting to you.
4. Breathe into your belly rather than your chest.
5. Bring a friendly facial expression to your body posture.
6. Gently fix your gaze on a single spot on the floor or close your eyes if you feel comfortable.

Now bring your attention to your breathing. Connect with your soothing rhythm-breathing, with your mind slowing down and body slowing down. Pay attention to your mind and body as you do this. Gradually get that sense of grounding with a sense of stilling and slowing, but also with an alert mind. Notice yourself becoming more grounded. (Pause.)

Now start connecting with your inner compassionate mind. Remember the wisdom that you have been developing in the course so far. We all have tricky brains and certain life experiences that have shaped how our minds and bodies work. Even though our tricky brains and life experiences have affected who we are, we also have minds that can learn how to change and make choices. We are developing the strength and commitment to help ourselves and others deal with the difficulties of life.

Acknowledge your courage and willingness to embark on this journey of learning, regardless of current circumstances. Acknowledge yourself for being open to learning and growing. You have the courage to stretch your boundaries, even if it's difficult, tricky, and scary. It's scary for everyone. Acknowledge yourself for being here exactly as you are.

You might do this in the form of a wish, something like:

- May I accept myself in this moment of learning exactly as I am.
- May I give myself all the support and all the kindness I need in this moment.
- May I accept all of my difficulties and doubts with compassion.
- May I give myself all the compassion I need in this moment.

Remember why we are in this group: to work on ways to be helpful to ourselves, to support others as best we can on their journey, and to be open to the helpfulness of others.

As we bring this practice of developing our compassionate intention to a close, connect with your body again. Feel your body in the chair in this moment. Slowly start to come back into the room, and open your eyes when you are ready.

Deepening Compassion for the Self

Aims:

- Deepen compassion for the self.
- Learn techniques that can be used to switch to compassionate self.

DOI: 10.4324/9781003607564-10

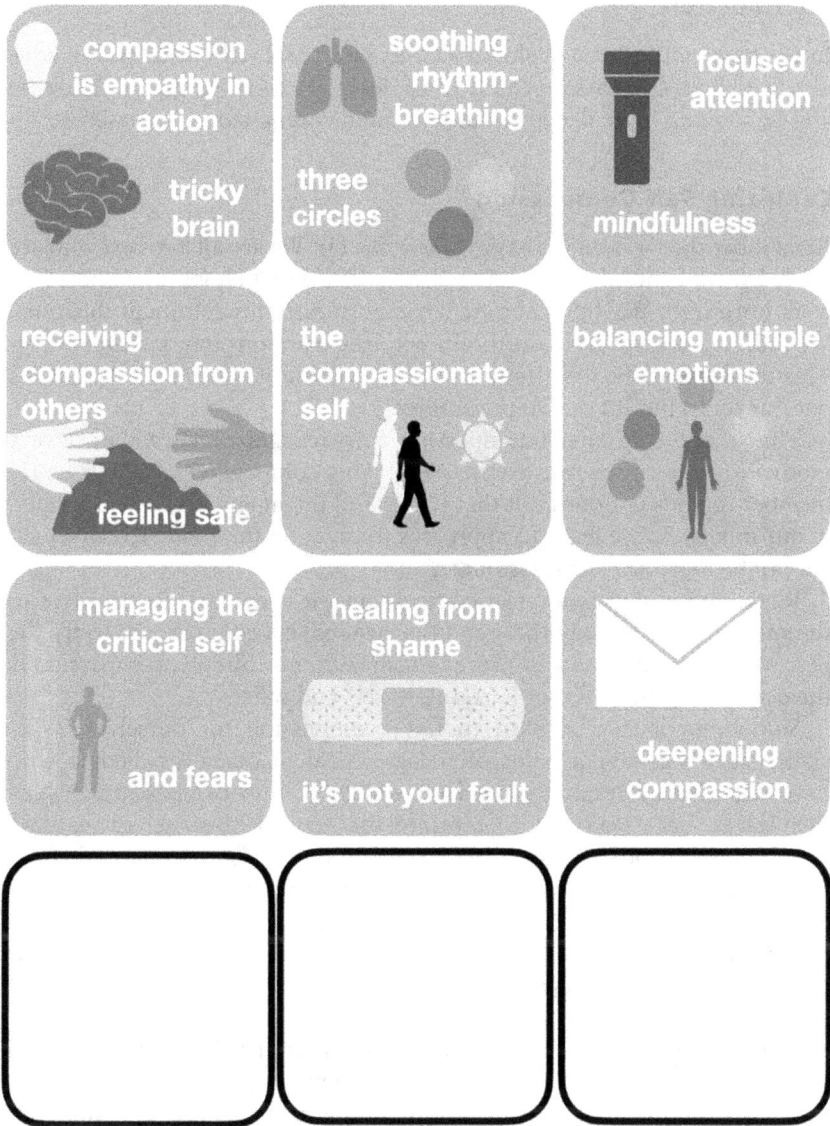

Figure 9 A visual representation of module 9 of 12.

Introduction

In the past modules we explored shame, guilt, and self-criticism. We have also seen how compassion can help us deal with those emotions. Now we will be looking more deeply at how to build compassion for ourselves.

Exploring Self Compassion

Remember the wisdom we have gained this far. We are all humans who are made by our genes that we didn't choose. We didn't choose the bodies we were born into. We didn't choose to be born into this culture at this time. We didn't choose to have our brain with the emotions that it's capable of. This means that the first step in self-compassion is to remember that it's not our fault, but it's our responsibility.

The second step in self-compassion is to recognize that we all have a motivation for caring and compassion. This compassion can help us remember that it's not our fault that tricky and threat emotions get activated in our minds. As we learn to apply this motivation for caring to ourselves, we can be more self-compassionate.

Remember our definition of compassion—it is that we are sensitive to the suffering of self and others and that we make a commitment to try the best we can to alleviate and prevent such suffering. Simply, compassion is the desire to be helpful, not harmful, to self and others.

Sometimes it can be hard to have compassion for ourselves, especially when we have a habit of being critical of ourselves. People who have experienced trauma often have difficulty with compassion toward themselves. Let's really try to tap into the version of ourselves that can be self-compassionate and respect our unique situation. What is this like? Like with other things we have learned in group, self-compassion will get easier with practice.

Let's work more to deepen compassion for ourselves. Here are a few exercises that you can try:

- Compassionate letter-writing: Turn to Handout 9.1. Write a letter to yourself from a compassionate point of view.
- Compassionate flash cards: Turn to Handout 9.2. Come up with compassionate statements to use in the future when you need them

Soft-landings are also exercises that can help you feel more compassion for yourself. Remember, it is easiest to feel self-compassion when in the soothing system.

Compassionate Letter

1. **Think** about something that makes you feel shame, self-critical, or not good enough.
2. **Notice** how it makes you feel.
3. **Activate** your compassionate-self.
4. **Write** a compassionate letter to yourself.

Dear _____,

_____

_____

_____

_____

_____

_____

_____

_____

_____

_____

_____

_____

From _____

Handout 9.1 Compassionate Letter-Writing

Compassionate Flashcards

Write down three or four really helpful statements, ideas, or actions that
would help you feel compassion during a difficult time.

Handout 9.2 Compassionate Flash Cards

Reviewing Compassion Process

Module 1: Dayroom fight, level drop, anger/anxiety, thinking loops; trick brain, "not my fault but my responsibility"

Module 2: Jordan's red circle scenario (anger); three circles, soothing rhythm-breathing

Module 3: Jordan's rumination on level drop, lingering anger; attention (flashlight), soothing rhythm-breathing

Module 4: Jordan's continuing threat mode; feelings safe through secure place/compassionate other imagery

Module 5: Jordan intentionally shifts to compassion; self-compassion in action (wisdom, strength, commitment)

Module 6: Jordan's dayroom situation produces multiple emotions; compassionate self understands and balances emotions

Module 7: Jordan's self-criticism; understanding inner critic and turning to growth through compassion

Module 8: Jordan's shame from yelling at staff; compassion to switch to guilt and remedy situation

Now let's think of how to apply what we have been learning today to Jordan's situation. As Jordan feels upset, he remembers that there are many ways to increase self-compassion.

What have we learned in this module that might help Jordan?

Notes

Between-Session Practice

Generating Compassion

We prepare to develop our compassionate intention:

1. Sit with a straight back. Keep your head upright and your shoulders in line with your hips. Place your feet flat on the floor.
2. Lift your shoulders up and slightly backward.
3. Find a comfortable position for your hands that will not be distracting to you.
4. Breathe into your belly rather than your chest.
5. Bring a friendly facial expression to your body posture.
6. Gently fix your gaze on a single spot on the floor or close your eyes if you feel comfortable.

Now bring your attention to your breathing. Connect with your soothing rhythm-breathing, with your mind slowing down and body slowing down. Pay attention to your mind and body as you do this. Gradually get that sense of grounding with a sense of stilling and slowing, but also with an alert mind. Notice yourself becoming more grounded. (Longer pause.)

Now start connecting with your inner compassionate mind. Remember the wisdom that you have been developing in the course so far. We all have tricky brains and certain life experiences that have shaped how our minds and bodies work. Even though our tricky brains and life experiences have affected who we are, we also have minds that can learn how to change and make choices. We are developing the strength and commitment to help ourselves and others deal with the difficulties of life.

Acknowledge your courage and willingness to embark on this journey of learning, regardless of current circumstances. Acknowledge yourself for being open to learning and growing. You have the courage to stretch your boundaries, even if it's difficult, tricky, and scary. It's scary for everyone. Acknowledge yourself for being here exactly as you are.

You might do this in the form of a wish, something like:

- May I accept myself in this moment of learning exactly as I am.
- May I give myself all the support and all the kindness I need in this moment.
- May I accept all of my difficulties and doubts with compassion.
- May I give myself all the compassion I need in this moment.

Gently ask yourself, "[Name], what do you want to take home from to-day's session?" Think about what lessons from this session will be the most helpful to you. Listen to whatever arises with curiosity.

Remember why we are in this group: to work on ways to be helpful to ourselves, to support others as best we can on their journey, and to be open to the helpfulness of others. Silently repeat these three flows of compassion back to yourself.

As we bring this practice of developing our compassionate intention to a close, connect with your body again. Feel your body in the chair in this moment. Slowly start to come back into the room, and open your eyes when you are ready.

Module 10

Compassionate Assertiveness

Aims:

- Learn what assertiveness is and what it is not.
- Explore how assertiveness ties into the strength and authority of compassion.
- Practice how we can say no with assertive communication.

DOI: 10.4324/9781003607564-11

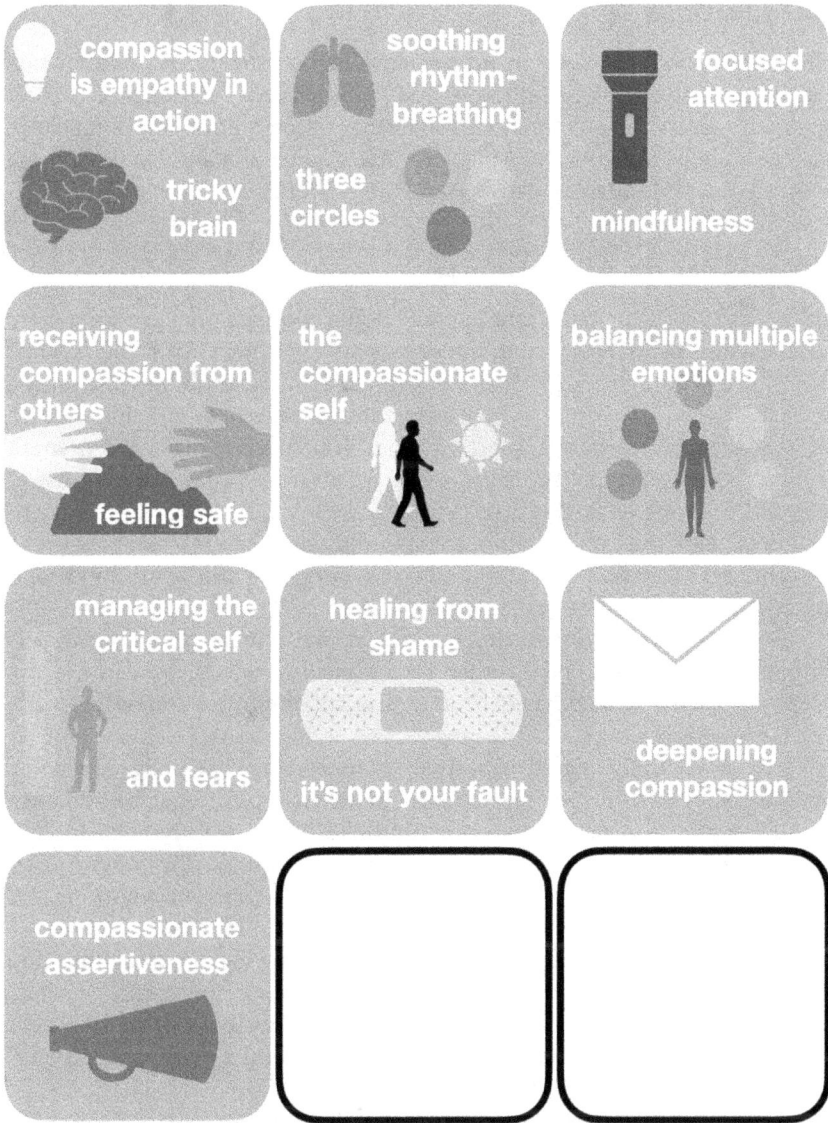

Figure 10 A visual representation of module 10 of 12.

Introduction

We have now spent time in group working to strengthen our compassionate self. Our compassionate self is very helpful. It can help us to feel grounded. It can also help create balance between all our emotions. So in this module, we're going to build on these compassionate self skills some more. We will do this by focusing on compassionate assertiveness.

Compassionate Assertiveness

Being assertive is an important part of having compassion. Compassionate assertiveness is not aggression, nor is it about "giving in" or being submissive. Compassionate assertiveness is learning to be clear about your values, wishes, wants, and needs. Compassionate assertiveness is being able to ask for these things or speak up for them. It helps us to have the strength and authority to say no to others when we need to. Compassionate assertiveness is giving clear and direct messages while also being open to critical feedback from others without responding defensively. Compassionate assertiveness is a skill that takes some practice. We will learn about and practice this skill today.

When we are compassionately assertive, we first try to notice what is happening inside us. Then, rather than attacking others, we can make a clear request for what we need. Automatic and impulsive responses can to lead us to attacks.

With a compassionately assertive response, you begin by describing what's happening inside of you rather than attacking. Imagine someone criticizes you. You might say something like "I can see my behavior has irritated or upset you. That was not my intention, so I'm sorry." This response is a good example of being thoughtful about our emotions and what the other person is feeling.

When we are assertive, we pay attention to our facial expressions and our voice tones. Both facial expressions and voice tones can be quite threatening to others when left unchecked. Being aware of them is another way to be thoughtful about what the other person is feeling and responding compassionately.

When we are assertive, we show our willingness to listen to the other person and communicate with the intent of understanding them. As we do this, we try to come to a compromise that works for both.

Assertiveness involves many components. Let's take a look at Handout 10.1 to see some examples of what assertiveness is.

Asking for What We Need Using Compassionate Assertiveness

Now, let's look at Handout 10.2 and start by thinking about a situation in which you may normally avoid asking for what you need. This may be a recent situation where you have been asked to do something and you said yes—but in fact you wanted to say no. This may be a situation where you were not assertive, but perhaps you were submissive/passive or maybe even aggressive.

Think of your own situation where you would need to use compassionate assertiveness. Think of a situation where you would typically avoid asking for what you need. Turn to Handout 10.2 write down what you might do from a compassionate perspective.

Let's imagine a situation where you would have to use compassionate assertiveness. You have a doctor's appointment tomorrow that you have been waiting for a while. Your friend calls you and wants you to help her with some easy to do chore at the same time tomorrow. You want to say no because the appointment is very important to you. Try to notice what happens in the body when you think about saying no. This would be a time to switch into slower breathing, grounding, and focusing on your compassionate intention (activate the soothing system). Think about how difficult it will be to say no to your friend. Think of what your compassionate self would tell you. How would you respond to your friend using compassionate assertiveness? Remember those steps. Would you use:

- An aggressive response?
- A passive or submissive response?
- A compassionately assertive response?

Take a moment to write your responses down in Handout 10.3. Write down what the outcome might be with each approach. For example, how might you feel if you respond in each way? How might your friend react if you respond in each way?

Remember the motivation of the compassionate self is to be understanding, respectful, and helpful to ourselves while listening and trying to meet the needs of others.

Components of Compassionate Assertiveness

ASSERTIVENESS

- is confidence
- is respect, for yourself and others
- is the ability to express concerns and needs
- is recognizing where another person is coming from
- is NOT allowing threat emotions to take over
- allows us to acknowledge our mistakes without feeling critical
- allows us to disagree with others without feeling attacked or shamed
- allows us to ask for and accept help
- is being genuinely empathetic to ourselves and others
- takes practice
- _____
- _____
- _____

Handout 10.1 Components of Compassionate Assertiveness

Reflections of the Compassionate-Self

• **Think** of a situation when you would normally avoid asking for what your need.

_____

• **Activate** your compassionate-self.
  • Move into your compassion body posture
  • slow your breathing, thinking "mind slowing down" and "body slowing down"

From your compassionate-self perspective...

• **What are my feelings in this situation?**

_____

_____

• **What are my needs in this situation?**

_____

_____

• **From my compassionate-self perspective, what would I like to say and do?**

_____

_____

Remember the motivation of the compassionate-self: to be understanding, respectful and helpful to ourselves while listening and trying to meet the needs of others.

Handout 10.2 Reflections of the Compassionate Self

Exploring Ways to Respond to Others

Example: You have a doctor appointment tomorrow. Your friend calls you and wants you to help her with some easy-to-do chore at the same time tomorrow. You want to say "no" because this appointment is very important.

An aggressive response:

_____

_____

Outcome:_____

A passive or submissive response:

_____

_____

Outcome:_____

A compassionately-assertive response:

_____

_____

Outcome:_____

Handout 10.3 Exploring Ways to Respond to Others

Reviewing Compassion Process

Module 1: Dayroom fight, level drop, anger/anxiety, thinking loops; trick brain, "not my fault but my responsibility"

Module 2: Jordan's red circle scenario (anger); three circles, soothing rhythm-breathing

Module 3: Jordan's rumination on level drop, lingering anger; attention (flashlight), soothing rhythm-breathing

Module 4: Jordan's continuing threat mode; feelings safe through secure place/compassionate other imagery

Module 5: Jordan intentionally shifts to compassion; self-compassion in action (wisdom, strength, commitment)

Module 6: Jordan's dayroom situation produces multiple emotions; compassionate self understands and balances emotions

Module 7: Jordan's self-criticism; understanding inner critic and turning to growth through compassion

Module 8: Jordan's shame from yelling at staff; compassion to switch to guilt and remedy situation

Module 9: A concrete exercise for Jordan's compassionate self; compassionate letter-writing

Let's apply what we learned today to Jordan. Jordan tries to use compassionate assertiveness to improve his situation and communicate his needs. Jordan was really angry when his level was dropped, so he asked if he could call his friend. When asked why, he explained that his level was dropped and he is distressed about it, so he would like to talk to his friend. Here, Jordan is being assertive and expressing his needs. The staff understand and allow him to call his friend.

Right then, another patient, Taylor, asks to use the phone. Jordan figures that if Taylor needs the phone more than him, then he will think of letting him go first. Here, Jordan is being compassionate. So Jordan asks Taylor why he needs the phone. Taylor explains that he already called his sister three times today but wants to call her again.

Based on what we have learned in this module, what should Jordan do?

Notes

Between-Session Practice

Generating Compassion

We prepare to develop our compassionate intention:

1. Sit with a straight back. Keep your head upright and your shoulders in line with your hips. Place your feet flat on the floor.
2. Lift your shoulders up and slightly backward.
3. Find a comfortable position for your hands that will not be distracting to you.
4. Breathe into your belly rather than your chest.
5. Bring a friendly facial expression to your body posture.
6. Gently fix your gaze on a single spot on the floor or close your eyes if you feel comfortable.

Now bring your attention to your breathing. Connect with your soothing rhythm-breathing, with your mind slowing down and body slowing down. Pay attention to your mind and body as you do this. Gradually get that sense of grounding with a sense of stilling and slowing, but also with an alert mind. Notice yourself becoming more grounded. (Longer pause.)

Now start connecting with your inner compassionate mind. Remember the wisdom that you have been developing in the course so far. We all have tricky brains and certain life experiences that have shaped how our minds and bodies work. Even though our tricky brains and life experiences have affected who we are, we also have minds that can learn how to change and make choices. We are developing the strength and commitment to help ourselves and others deal with the difficulties of life.

Acknowledge your courage and willingness to embark on this journey of learning, regardless of current circumstances. Acknowledge yourself for being open to learning and growing. You have the courage to stretch your boundaries, even if it's difficult, tricky, and scary. It's scary for everyone. Acknowledge yourself for being here exactly as you are.

You might do this in the form of a wish, something like:

- May I accept myself in this moment of learning exactly as I am.
- May I give myself all the support and all the kindness I need in this moment.
- May I accept all of my difficulties and doubts with compassion.
- May I give myself all the compassion I need in this moment.

Gently ask yourself, "[Name], what do you want to take home from to-day's session?" Think about what lessons from this session will be the most helpful to you. Listen to whatever arises with curiosity.

Remember why we are in this group: to work on ways to be helpful to ourselves, to support others as best we can on their journey, and to be open to the helpfulness of others. Silently repeat these three flows of compassion back to yourself.

As we bring this practice of developing our compassionate intention to a close, connect with your body again. Feel your body in the chair in this moment. Slowly start to come back into the room, and open your eyes when you are ready.

Forgiveness

Aims:

- Explore the flow of compassion for others.
- Identify ways to be compassionate to others.
- Learn what forgiveness is.
- Explore ways to develop compassion for people we don't like.

DOI: 10.4324/9781003607564-12

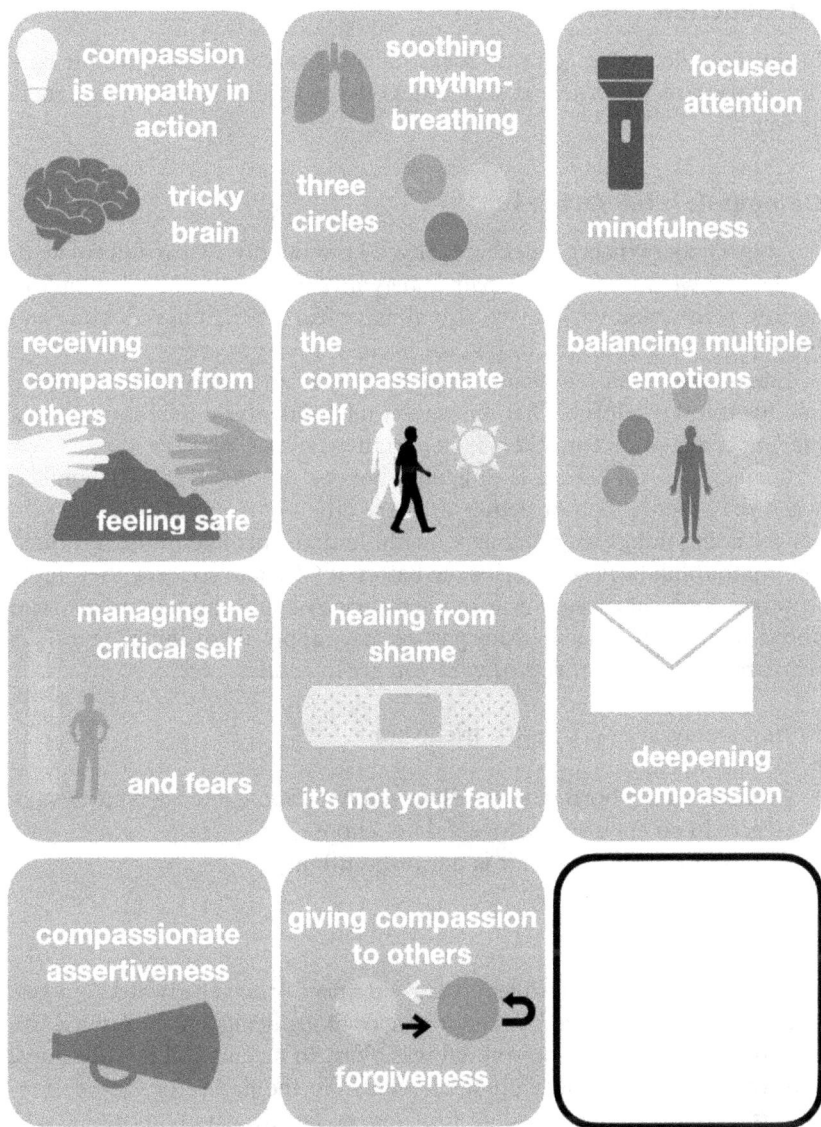

Figure 11 A visual representation of module 11 of 12.

Introduction

In this module, we're going to focus on compassion for others. One part of compassion for others is forgiveness. So we will focus on forgiveness as well.

Compassion for Others

Nobody chooses their gender, ethnicity, or personality. We are all trying to do the best we can to manage pain and avoid suffering. We all have built-in desires, wants, and wishes. We also all have fears. We all have a body and brain that's been built for us but not by us.

Life is filled with moments of suffering. We can be moved by suffering and want to be helpful. That movement might involve different emotions. Having compassion for others is important.

Compassion for others is difficult when we are involved in a conflict, when the other person or people are very different from us, or when others are doing things we don't agree with. In moments like these, it is often helpful to think back to some of the basics of CFT and see how they apply to others and ourselves. For a moment, try to apply the statements I am about to read to others. More particularly, apply these things to others who are different from you or who you are in conflict with.

- All humans are born with a tricky brain.
- We all suffer.
- All humans are born with genes we did not choose and then have experiences in an environment we did not choose.
- This is not our fault, but it is our responsibility.

Forgiveness

Forgiveness is a decision to let go of resentment or anger toward someone else. Forgiveness is not about condoning or liking being hurt or bullied. We are *not* saying what the person did was okay. In meaningful relationships, forgiveness is part of developing closeness. So the nature of the relationship is crucial to understanding forgiveness. Forgiveness is more likely if we are assertive and use conflict resolution skills. Again, forgiveness is not a submissive act. Turn to Handout 11.1 to read through what forgiveness is and what it is not.

Next, work through Handout 11.2, to practice having compassion for another in a difficult situation. This handout will show you how your compassionate self helps you care for others.

To further practice forgiveness, turn to Handout 11.3. Think of some-one you would like to forgive. Remember that forgiveness is not easy, but it is a way through which we can heal and move on. Write a forgiveness letter to the person you want to forgive.

Empathy

Being mindful of others helps us to become sensitive to our own feelings, to the feelings of others, and to tolerate when our feelings are distressing and unpleasant. This is empathy.

Empathy can be defined as the capacity to recognize feelings and un-derstand what is happening within another person and why that might be so, without judging them. The more we can understand the emotions of another, the easier it is for us to know how to best interact with them. Self-empathy is understanding that we have a tricky brain and understand-ing what we think and what we feel.

Sympathy is our own emotional reaction to another person's distress. It may be the same or different from the feelings of the other person. With affective empathy, we tune in to the other person's feelings, knowing they originate in them and not in us.

Defining Forgiveness

IS:

- Is a way to move on from past hurt and pain.

- Allows us to let go of anger, resentment, and vengeful feelings.

- Part of developing closeness in a relationship.

- More likely to happen if we have good assertiveness.

- Something that we do for ourselves—not for others.

- _____

- _____

- _____

IS NOT:

- Thinking the behavior of somebody else os okay or right.

- Staying close to someone who hurt you.

- Forgetting.

- Liking the person or needing to be friends with the person.

- A way to stop hurting.

- Easy.

- _____

- _____

- _____

Handout 11.1 Defining Forgiveness

Compassion for Others in Difficult Situations

Write down a situation when you were in conflict with another.
Next. activate vour compassionate-self and respond to the followina auestions:
What might the other person have felt?
What might the other person have thought?
What might the needs of the other person have been?
What intentions might the other person have had?
What are your compassionate wishes for the other person?

Handout 11.2 Compassion for Others in Difficult Situations

Forgiveness Letter

Think of someone you would like to forgive. Remember forgiveness is not always easy, but a way we can heal and move on. In the space below, write a forgiveness letter to this person.

_____

_____

_____

_____

_____

_____

_____

_____

_____

_____

_____

_____

_____

_____

_____

_____

_____

_____

Handout 11.3 Forgiveness Letter

Reviewing Compassion Process

Module 1: Dayroom fight, level drop, anger/anxiety, thinking loops; trick brain, "not my fault but my responsibility"
Module 2: Jordan's red circle scenario (anger); three circles, soothing rhythm-breathing
Module 3: Jordan's rumination on level drop, lingering anger; attention (flashlight), soothing rhythm-breathing
Module 4: Jordan's continuing threat mode; feelings safe through secure place/compassionate other imagery
Module 5: Jordan intentionally shifts to compassion; self-compassion in action (wisdom, strength, commitment)
Module 6: Jordan's dayroom situation produces multiple emotions; compassionate self understands and balances emotions
Module 7: Jordan's self-criticism; understanding inner critic and turning to growth through compassion
Module 8: Jordan's shame from yelling at staff; compassion to switch to guilt and remedy situation
Module 9: A concrete exercise for Jordan's compassionate self; compassionate letter-writing
Module 10: Jordan wants to call his friend, someone else wants to use the phone; compassionate assertiveness

Now let's think of how to apply what we have been learning today to Jordan's situation. After getting in trouble, Jordan's automatic reaction was to be angry. He yelled at staff for misunderstanding what happened. He blamed the new patient for getting him in trouble. But then Jordan remembers to try to have compassion for the new patient. He imagines what the new patient must be feeling. He remembers how hard it was to be a new patient at the hospital. Jordan imagines the new patient is probably feeling scared and overwhelmed.

Based on what we have learned in this module, what should Jordan do?

Notes

Between-Session Practice

Experiencing the Flows of Compassion

We prepare to develop our compassionate intention:

- Sit with a straight back. Keep your head upright and your shoulders in line with your hips. Place your feet flat on the floor.
- Lift your shoulders up and slightly backward.
- Find a comfortable position for your hands that will not be distracting to you.
- Breathe into your belly rather than your chest.
- Bring a friendly facial expression to your body posture.
- Gently fix your gaze on a single spot on the floor or close your eyes if you feel comfortable.

Now bring your attention to your breathing. Connect with your soothing rhythm-breathing, with your mind slowing down and body slowing down. Pay attention to your mind and body as you do this. Gradually get that sense of grounding with a sense of stilling and slowing, but also with an alert mind. Notice yourself becoming more grounded. (Longer pause.)

Now start connecting with your inner compassionate mind. Remember the wisdom that you have been developing in the course so far. We all have tricky brains and certain life experiences that have shaped how our minds and bodies work. Even though our tricky brains and life experiences have affected who we are, we also have minds that can learn how to change and make choices. We are developing the strength and commitment to help ourselves and others deal with the difficulties of life.

Acknowledge your courage and willingness to embark on this journey of learning, regardless of current circumstances. Acknowledge yourself for being open to learning and growing. You have the courage to stretch your boundaries, even if it's difficult, tricky, and scary. It's scary for everyone. Acknowledge yourself for being here exactly as you are. You might do this in the form of a wish, something like:

- May I accept myself in this moment of learning exactly as I am.
- May I give myself all the support and all the kindness I need in this moment.
- May I accept all of my difficulties and doubts with compassion.
- May I give myself all the compassion I need in this moment.

Gently ask yourself, "[Name], what do you want to take home from to-day's session?" Think about what lessons from this session will be the most helpful to you. Listen to whatever arises with curiosity.

Remember why we are in this group: to work on ways to be helpful to ourselves, to support others as best we can on their journey, and to be open to the helpfulness of others. Silently repeat these three flows of compassion back to yourself.

Envisioning a Compassionate Future

Aims:

- Revisit the journey that the group has been on.
- Create prevention and emergency strategies for the future.
- Begin to think about what a compassion future would look like.

DOI: 10.4324/9781003607564-13

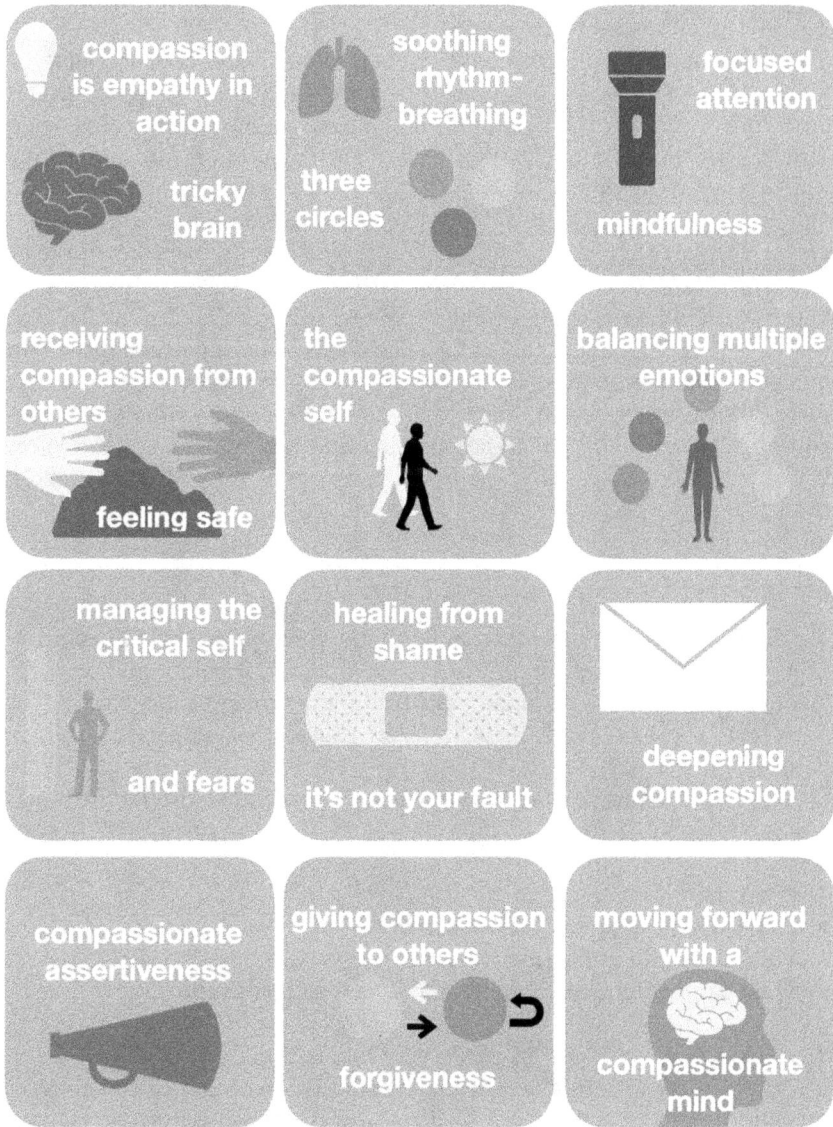

Figure 12 A visual representation of module 12 of 12.

Introduction

This is the final module. You have learned so much and come so far. Our focus in this module will be on creating prevention and emergency strategies. Let's remember the definition of compassion. Part of it is alleviating suffering when it occurs. Another part of the definition is also preventing suffering when we can.

Prevention and Emergency Strategies

Today we will be reflecting on the exercises, strategies, and practices that you have been learning in this group. The aim is to see if you can turn them into prevention strategies. Try to come up with strategies for each of the three flows of compassion. Turn to Handout 12.1 and write down when you might need each flow of compassion and how you can access each. Which areas are easier to come up with strategies for? Which are more challenging for you?

Envisioning a Compassionate Future

We thank you for the time and efforts that you have put into this compassion focused therapy group. You have the wisdom, strength, and commitment to move forward with compassion. Take a moment and acknowledge the efforts you have made as well. From your compassionate self, thank yourself.

Let's take a moment to reflect on what we have experienced together as a group. Ask yourself:

- What did I learn in group?
- How have I changed since I started?
- What did I find difficult in the group?
- What can help me to continue to practicing compassion?

Then to end, we will go through a final meditation "Envisioning a Compassionate Future." As always, this exercise is at the end of this module for you to refer back to in the future. After the exercise, turn to Hanout 12.2 and write down how you envision your compassionate future in this moment.

We recommend you keep your CFT workbook so you can refer back to all you've learned. We again thank you for your participation in this group. We wish you the best of luck in your future!

To continue your compassion journey, check out the book *Relating to Voices using Compassion Focused Therapy: A Self-Help Companion*, by Dr. Heriot-Maitland.

Prevention and Emergency Strategies

Self-Compassion	
In which situations will I need self-compassion the most? • _____ • _____ • _____ • _____	**What are things I can do during these times to access self-compassion?** • _____ • _____ • _____ • _____
Compassion for Others	
In which situations will I need to give compassion to others? • _____ • _____ • _____ • _____	**What are things I can do during these times to give compassion to others?** • _____ • _____ • _____ • _____
Compassion from Others	
In which situations will I need to receive compassion from others? • _____ • _____ • _____ • _____	**What are things I can do during these times to receive compassion from others?** • _____ • _____ • _____ • _____

Handout 12.1 Prevention and Emergency Strategies

Envisioning a Compassionate Future

Imagine your future as your most compassionate self. You will experience many ups and downs but you continue to practice compassion. What is your future self like? What does your life look like? What dreams or goals have you accomplished?

Write or draw this future below.

Handout 12.2 Envisioning a Compassionate Future

Reviewing Compassion Process

Module 1: Dayroom fight, level drop, anger/anxiety, thinking loops; trick brain, "not my fault but my responsibility"

Module 2: Jordan's red circle scenario (anger); three circles, soothing rhythm-breathing

Module 3: Jordan's rumination on level drop, lingering anger; attention (flashlight), soothing rhythm-breathing

Module 4: Jordan's continuing threat mode; feelings safe through secure place/compassionate other imagery

Module 5: Jordan intentionally shifts to compassion; self-compassion in action (wisdom, strength, commitment)

Module 6: Jordan's dayroom situation produces multiple emotions; compassionate self understands and balances emotions

Module 7: Jordan's self-criticism; understanding inner critic and turning to growth through compassion

Module 8: Jordan's shame from yelling at staff; compassion to switch to guilt and remedy situation

Module 9: A concrete exercise for Jordan's compassionate self; compassionate letter-writing

Module 10: Jordan wants to call his friend, someone else wants to use the phone; compassionate assertiveness

Module 11: Jordan blames new patient for dayroom situation; forgiveness, understanding new patient, letting go of bitterness

Let's try to envision a compassionate future using what Jordan has learned. Jordan thinks of the wisdom he has. He knows that we were born with a tricky brain. He knows he has life experiences he didn't choose. Even though he didn't choose them, his brain and life experiences shape who he is. That isn't his fault. But it is his responsibility to do what he can with the life he has. He can continue to develop the strength and commitment to help himself and others deal with life and inner difficulties. Jordan commits to continue practicing compassion. He uses soothing rhythm-breathing to move into the green circle. He uses mindfulness and imagery to notice and balance his emotions. He uses exercises like compassionate letter-writing to further develop self-compassion As Jordan applies what he has learned he is on a path to a compassionate future, just like you.

Final Practice

Envisioning a Compassionate Future

Today, we will be imagining what a compassionate future looks like for us. To begin, we will engage our compassionate body posture.

- Sit with a straight back. Keep your head upright and your shoulders in line with your hips. Place your feet flat on the floor.
- Lift your shoulders up and slightly backward.
- Find a comfortable position for your hands that will not be distracting to you.
- Breathe into your belly rather than your chest.
- Bring a friendly facial expression to your body posture.
- Gently fix your gaze on a single spot on the floor or close your eyes if you feel comfortable.

Now, imagine that you will be your most compassionate self from now on. Being compassionate has become your greatest goal. You will experience many ups and downs as you pursue your goal. However, you will continue to move in a compassionate direction.

Imagine your most compassionate self in five years. Imagine that you have been strong, wise, and committed to compassionate living. You remember the fragility of being human and bravely engage with suffering.

Now, consider these questions:

- What qualities will you have developed in five years?
- What will the circumstances of your life look like?
- What dreams or goals will you have accomplished?
- Notice any feelings or sensations that arise when thinking about life as your most compassionate self in five years.

Next, take a moment to consider how you will have changed in ten years.

- What qualities will you have developed?
- What will the circumstances of your life look like?
- What dreams or goals will you have accomplished?
- Notice any feelings or sensations that arise when thinking about life as your most compassionate self in ten years.

As we bring this practice to a close, connect with your body again. Feel your body in the chair in this moment. Slowly start to come back into the room, and open your eyes when you are ready.

Index

For Product Safety Concerns and Information please contact our EU
representative GPSR@taylorandfrancis.com
Taylor & Francis Verlag GmbH, Kaufingerstraße 24, 80331 München, Germany

www.ingramcontent.com/pod-product-compliance
Lightning Source LLC
Chambersburg PA
CBHW052012270326
41929CB00015B/2891

* 9 7 8 1 0 0 3 8 6 3 9 0 8 *